MW01285735

GOVERNMENT PROCEDURES AND OPERATIONS

DEBT LIMIT IMPASSES

ANALYSES AND EFFECTS

GOVERNMENT PROCEDURES AND OPERATIONS

Additional books in this series can be found on Nova's website under the Series tab.

Additional e-books in this series can be found on Nova's website under the e-book tab.

GOVERNMENT PROCEDURES AND OPERATIONS

DEBT LIMIT IMPASSES

ANALYSES AND EFFECTS

PHIL FRAZIER
EDITOR

nova publishers
New York

Copyright © 2016 by Nova Science Publishers, Inc.

All rights reserved. No part of this book may be reproduced, stored in a retrieval system or transmitted in any form or by any means: electronic, electrostatic, magnetic, tape, mechanical photocopying, recording or otherwise without the written permission of the Publisher.

We have partnered with Copyright Clearance Center to make it easy for you to obtain permissions to reuse content from this publication. Simply navigate to this publication's page on Nova's website and locate the "Get Permission" button below the title description. This button is linked directly to the title's permission page on copyright.com. Alternatively, you can visit copyright.com and search by title, ISBN, or ISSN.

For further questions about using the service on copyright.com, please contact:
Copyright Clearance Center
Phone: +1-(978) 750-8400   Fax: +1-(978) 750-4470   E-mail: info@copyright.com.

NOTICE TO THE READER

The Publisher has taken reasonable care in the preparation of this book, but makes no expressed or implied warranty of any kind and assumes no responsibility for any errors or omissions. No liability is assumed for incidental or consequential damages in connection with or arising out of information contained in this book. The Publisher shall not be liable for any special, consequential, or exemplary damages resulting, in whole or in part, from the readers' use of, or reliance upon, this material. Any parts of this book based on government reports are so indicated and copyright is claimed for those parts to the extent applicable to compilations of such works.

Independent verification should be sought for any data, advice or recommendations contained in this book. In addition, no responsibility is assumed by the publisher for any injury and/or damage to persons or property arising from any methods, products, instructions, ideas or otherwise contained in this publication.

This publication is designed to provide accurate and authoritative information with regard to the subject matter covered herein. It is sold with the clear understanding that the Publisher is not engaged in rendering legal or any other professional services. If legal or any other expert assistance is required, the services of a competent person should be sought. FROM A DECLARATION OF PARTICIPANTS JOINTLY ADOPTED BY A COMMITTEE OF THE AMERICAN BAR ASSOCIATION AND A COMMITTEE OF PUBLISHERS.

Additional color graphics may be available in the e-book version of this book.

Library of Congress Cataloging-in-Publication Data

ISBN: 978-1-63484-335-5

Published by Nova Science Publishers, Inc. † New York

CONTENTS

PREFACE

The gross federal debt, which represents the federal government's total outstanding debt, consists of debt held by the public and debt held in government accounts, also known as intragovernmental debt. Federal government borrowing increases for two primary reasons: (1) budget deficits and (2) investments of any federal government account surpluses in Treasury securities, as required by law. Nearly all of this debt is subject to the statutory limit. Treasury has yet to face a situation in which it was unable to pay its obligations as a result of reaching the debt limit. In the past, the debt limit has always been raised before the debt reached the limit. This book examines the possibility of the federal government reaching its statutory debt limit and not raising it, with a particular focus on government operations. First, the book explains the nature of the federal government's debt, the processes associated with federal borrowing, and historical events that may influence prospective actions. It also includes an analysis of what could happen if the federal government may no longer issue debt, has exhausted alternative sources of cash, and, therefore, depends on incoming receipts or other sources of funds to provide any cash needed to liquidate federal obligations. A discussion of the effects that prior debt limit impasses have had on the economy is also included. Finally, this book lays out considerations for increasing the debt limit under current policy and what impact fiscal policy could have on the debt limit going forward.

In: Debt Limit Impasses   ISBN: 978-1-63484-335-5
Editor: Phil Frazier   © 2016 Nova Science Publishers, Inc.

Chapter 1

REACHING THE DEBT LIMIT:
BACKGROUND AND POTENTIAL EFFECTS
ON GOVERNMENT OPERATIONS[*]

Mindy R. Levit, Clinton T. Brass,
Thomas J. Nicola and Dawn Nuschler

SUMMARY

The gross federal debt, which represents the federal government's total outstanding debt, consists of (1) debt held by the public and (2) debt held in government accounts, also known as intragovernmental debt. Federal government borrowing increases for two primary reasons: (1) budget deficits and (2) investments of any federal government account surpluses in Treasury securities, as required by law. Nearly all of this debt is subject to the statutory limit.

Treasury has yet to face a situation in which it was unable to pay its obligations as a result of reaching the debt limit. In the past, the debt limit has always been raised before the debt reached the limit. However, on several occasions Treasury took extraordinary actions to avoid reaching the limit which, as a result, affected the operations of certain programs. If the Secretary of the Treasury determines that the issuance of obligations of the United States may not be made without exceeding the public debt

---

[*] This is an edited, reformatted and augmented version of a Congressional Research Service publication R41633, prepared for Members and Committees of Congress, dated March 27, 2015.

limit, Treasury can make use of "extraordinary measures." Some of these measures require the Treasury Secretary to authorize a debt issuance suspension period.

Since 2011, the debt limit has been increased through provisions of four pieces of legislation. The debt limit was increased on August 2, 2011, as part of the Budget Control Act of 2011 (BCA; P.L. 112-25). The BCA also provided for two additional debt limit increases, which occurred in September 2011 and January 2012. On February 4, 2013, the statutory debt limit was suspended through May 18, 2013, as part of the No Budget, No Pay Act of 2013 (P.L. 113-3). On October 17, 2013, the debt limit was suspended again through February 7, 2014, as part of the Continuing Appropriations Act, 2014 (P.L. 113-46). On February 15, 2014, the debt limit was suspended for a third time through, March 15, 2015, as part of the Temporary Debt Limit Extension Act (P.L. 113- 83). Between the enactment of each of these legislative measures, Treasury used extraordinary measures to continue financing obligations. On May 19, 2013, February 8, 2014, and March 16, 2015, the debt limit was reinstated at a level which accommodated borrowing incurred during the suspension periods.

Budget outlays and revenue collections along with the funds contained in the extraordinary measures will affect the timing of when the debt limit is reached. If the debt limit is reached and Treasury is no longer able to issue federal debt, federal outlays would have to be decreased or federal revenues would have to be increased by a corresponding amount to cover the gap in what cannot be borrowed.

It is extremely difficult for Congress to effectively influence short-term fiscal and budgetary policy through action on legislation adjusting the debt limit. The need to raise (or lower) the limit during a session of Congress is driven by previous decisions regarding revenues and spending stemming from legislation enacted earlier in the session or in prior years. Nevertheless, the consideration of debt limit legislation often is viewed as an opportunity to reexamine fiscal and budgetary policy. Consequently, House and Senate action on legislation adjusting the debt limit is often complicated, hindered by policy disagreements, and subject to delay.

The federal government's statutory debt limit was reinstated on March 16, 2015, at a level that accommodated the borrowing incurred during the suspension period, which ended on March 15, 2015 (P.L. 113-83).[1] Treasury immediately began using its authority outside of its typical cash management practices to pay federal obligations to delay the date by which the debt limit would impede the federal government's ability to make timely payments on all of its obligations (through a debt issuance suspension period as well as other methods discussed in more detail later in this report). Similar actions have been taken previously. If these financing options are exhausted and Treasury is no longer able to pay for all federal obligations, some federal payments to creditors, vendors, contractors, state and local governments, beneficiaries, and other entities would be delayed or limited. This could result in significant economic and financial consequences that may have a lasting impact on federal programs and the federal government's ability to borrow in the future.

This report examines the possibility of the federal government reaching its statutory debt limit and not raising it, with a particular focus on government operations. First, the report explains the nature of the federal government's debt, the processes associated with federal borrowing, and historical events that may influence prospective actions. It also includes an analysis of what *could* happen if the federal government may no longer issue debt, has exhausted alternative sources of cash, and, therefore, depends on incoming receipts or other sources of funds to provide any cash needed to liquidate federal obligations.[2] A discussion of the effects that prior debt limit impasses have had on the economy is also included. Finally, this report lays out considerations for increasing the debt limit under current policy and what impact fiscal policy could have on the debt limit going forward.

FEDERAL GOVERNMENT DEBT AND THE DEBT LIMIT[3]

The gross federal debt, which represents the federal government's total outstanding debt, consists of:

- the debt held by the public and
- the debt held in government accounts, also known as intragovernmental debt.

Federal government borrowing increases for two primary reasons: (1) budget deficits and (2) investments of any federal government account surpluses in Treasury securities as required by law.[4]

The debt held by the public represents the total net amount borrowed from the public to cover the federal government's accumulated budget deficits. Annual budget deficits increase the debt held by the public by requiring the federal government to borrow additional funds to fulfill its commitments.

The debt held in government accounts represents the federal debt issued to certain accounts, primarily trust funds, such as those associated with Social Security, Medicare, and Unemployment Compensation. Generally, government account surpluses, which include trust fund surpluses, by law must be invested in special non-marketable federal government securities and thus are held in the form of federal debt.[5] Treasury periodically pays interest on the special securities held in a government account. Interest payments are typically paid in the form of additional special securities issued by Treasury to the trust funds, which also increases the amount of intragovernmental debt and federal debt subject to limit.

When a trust fund invests in U.S. Treasury securities, it effectively lends money to the rest of the government. The loan either reduces what the federal government must borrow from the public if the budget is in deficit, or reduces the amount of publicly held debt if the budget is in surplus. At the same time, the loan increases intragovernmental debt. The revenues exchanged for these securities then go into the General Fund of the Treasury and are indistinguishable from other cash in the General Fund. This cash may be used for any government spending purpose.[6]

Congress created a statutory debt limit in the Second Liberty Bond Act of 1917.[7] This development changed Treasury's borrowing process and assisted Congress in its efforts to exercise its constitutional prerogatives to control the federal government's fiscal outcomes. The debt limit also imposes a form of fiscal accountability that compels Congress and the President to take deliberate action to allow further federal borrowing if necessary.

Almost all of the federal government's borrowing is subject to a statutory limit.[8] From time to time, Congress has considered and adopted legislation to change or suspend this limit. Because the statutory limit applies to debt held by the public as well as intragovernmental debt, both budget deficits and government account surpluses may contribute to the federal government reaching the existing debt limit.

THE DEBT LIMIT AND THE TREASURY

Treasury's standard methods for financing federal activities can be disrupted when the level of federal debt nears its legal limit. If the limit prevents Treasury from issuing new debt to manage short-term cash flows or to finance an annual deficit, the government may be unable to obtain the cash needed to pay its bills. The limit may also prevent the government from issuing new debt in order to invest the surpluses of designated government accounts, such as federal trust funds. Treasury is caught between two requirements: the law that requires Treasury to pay the government's legal obligations or invest trust fund surpluses, on one hand, and the statutory debt limit which may prevent Treasury from issuing the debt to raise cash to pay obligations or make trust fund investments, on the other.[9]

The level of federal debt changes throughout the year due to fluctuations in revenue and outlays, regardless of whether or not the government has an annual surplus or deficit. Seasonal fluctuations could still require Treasury to sell debt even if the annual level of federal debt subject to limit does not increase (i.e., if the budget were balanced and trust funds were not in surplus). Even on a day-to-day basis, the level of federal debt can vary significantly. For example, Treasury issues large volumes of individual income tax refunds in February and March, because taxpayers expecting refunds tend to file early. On the other hand, Treasury tends to collect more revenue in April because taxpayers making payments tend to file closer to April 15.

Past Treasury Secretaries, when faced with a nearly binding debt ceiling, have used special strategies to handle cash and debt management responsibilities.[10] Since 1985, these measures have included

- suspending sales of nonmarketable debt (savings bonds, state and local government series, and other nonmarketable debt);
- trimming or delaying auctions of marketable securities;
- under-investing or disinvesting certain government funds (Social Security, Government Securities Investment Fund of the Federal Thrift Savings Plan, the Civil Service Retirement and Disability Trust Fund, Postal Service Retiree Health Benefit Fund, Exchange Stabilization Fund);[11] and
- exchanging Treasury securities for non-Treasury securities held by the Federal Financing Bank (FFB).

Under current law, if the Secretary of the Treasury determines that the issuance of obligations of the United States may not be made without exceeding the debt limit, a "debt issuance suspension period" may be determined.[12] This determination gives Treasury the authority to suspend investments in the Civil Service Retirement and Disability Trust Fund, Postal Service Retiree Health Benefit Fund, and the Government Securities Investment Fund (G-Fund) of the Federal Thrift Savings Plan. In addition, this gives Treasury the authority to prematurely redeem securities held by the Civil

Service Retirement and Disability Trust Fund and Postal Service Retiree Health Benefit Fund. Debt issuance suspension periods were previously in effect from November 15, 1995, through January 15, 1997; April 4 through April 16, 2002; May 16 through June 28, 2002; February 20 through May 27, 2003; May 16 through August 2, 2011; December 31, 2012, through February 4, 2013; May 20, 2013 to October 17, 2013; and February 10, 2014, to February 15, 2014. Most recently, a debt limit suspension period began on March 16, 2015, and is still currently in effect.

Past Treasury Actions to Postpone Reaching the Debt Limit

Treasury has yet to face a situation in which it was unable to pay its obligations as a result of reaching the debt limit. However, during debt limit impasses in 1985, 1995-1996, 2002, 2003, 2011, 2013, 2014, and 2015. Treasury took extraordinary actions to avoid reaching the debt limit and to meet the federal government's other obligations. Some of the actions Treasury took during these periods are briefly discussed below.[13]

Actions in 1985

In September 1985, the Treasury Department informed Congress that it had reached the statutory debt limit. As a result, Treasury had to take extraordinary measures to meet the government's cash requirements. Treasury used various internal transactions involving the Federal Financing Bank (FFB) and delayed public auctions of government debt. It also was unable to issue, or had to delay issuing, new short-term government securities to the Civil Service Retirement and Disability Trust Fund, the Social Security Trust Funds, and several smaller trust funds. In particular, new Treasury obligations could not be issued to the trust funds because doing so would have exceeded the debt limit. Treasury took the additional step of "disinvesting" the Civil Service Retirement and Disability Trust Fund, the Social Security Trust Funds, and several smaller trust funds by redeeming some trust fund securities earlier than usual. Premature redemption of these securities created room under the debt ceiling for Treasury to borrow sufficient cash from the public to pay other obligations, including November 1985 Social Security benefits.[14] The debt limit was subsequently temporarily increased on November 14, 1985 (P.L. 99-155) and permanently increased on December 12, 1985 (P.L. 99-177) from $1,824 billion to $2,079 billion.

As a result of the 1985 debt limit crisis, Congress subsequently authorized Treasury to alter its normal investment and redemption procedures for certain trust funds during a debt limit crisis. Such authority was not provided with respect to the Social Security Trust Funds. In addition, both P.L. 99-155 and P.L. 99-177 included provisions to require Treasury to restore any interest income lost to the trust funds as a result of delayed investments and early redemptions.

Actions in 1995-1996

During the debt limit crisis of 1995-1996, Treasury, once again, used nontraditional methods of financing, including some of the methods used during the 1985 crisis as well as not reinvesting some of the maturing Treasury securities held by the Exchange Stabilization Fund.[15] In early 1996, Treasury announced that it had insufficient cash to pay Social Security benefits for March 1996, because it was unable to issue new public debt.[16] To allow benefits to be paid in March 1996, Congress authorized Treasury to issue securities to the public in the amount needed to make the March 1996 benefit payments and specified that, on a temporary basis, those securities would not count against the debt limit (P.L. 104-103 and P.L. 104-115). In 1996, Congress passed P.L. 104-121 to increase the debt limit and, among other provisions, to codify Congress's understanding that the Secretary of the Treasury and other federal officials are not authorized to use Social Security and Medicare funds for debt management purposes, except when necessary to provide for the payment of benefits or administrative expenses of the programs.

Actions in 2002-2003

During periods in 2002 and 2003 (from April 4 through April 16, 2002; from May 16 through June 28, 2002; and from February 20 through May 27, 2003), Treasury again took actions to avoid reaching the debt limit. These actions included utilizing certain trust fund assets and suspending the sale of securities to certain trust funds. The debt limit was permanently increased on June 28, 2002 (P.L. 107-199), from $5,950 billion to $6,400 billion and on May 27, 2003 (P.L. 108-24), from $6,400 billion to $7,384 billion.

Actions in 2009

Treasury used another tool in 2009 to cope with the debt limit without declaring a debt issuance suspension period. Specifically, Treasury used a program that was originally established as an alternative method for the

Federal Reserve (Fed) to increase its assistance to the financial sector during the financial downturn, the Supplementary Financing Program (SFP). The SFP was announced on September 17, 2008. Under the SFP, Treasury temporarily auctioned more new securities than were needed to finance government operations and deposited the proceeds at the Fed. Beginning in January 2009, Treasury generally held $200 billion at the Fed under this program. When debt subject to limit approached the statutory debt limit around October 2009, however, Treasury withdrew all but $5 billion from the Fed to create room under the debt ceiling. Once the debt limit was raised on February 12, 2010, from $12,394 billion to $14,294 billion (P.L. 111-139), Treasury began increasing the balances held at the Fed back to $200 billion by issuing new debt to the public. As the debt limit was approached again, the SFP was reduced from $200 billion on February 2, 2011, to $5 billion on March 3, 2011, and to $0 on August 3, 2011.[17]

Treasury Actions Surrounding the Debt Limit Since 2011

Actions in 2011

Beginning in January 2011, Treasury again took actions to avoid reaching the debt limit and began notifying Congress of its intentions. On January 6, 2011, Treasury Secretary Geithner sent a letter to Congress stating that Treasury had the ability to delay the date by which the debt limit would be reached by utilizing similar methods used during past crises, including declaring a debt issuance suspension period, if necessary.[18] On May 2, 2011, Secretary Geithner issued another letter to Congress reiterating that the debt limit would be reached no later than May 16, 2011, but that the use of extraordinary measures would extend Treasury's ability to meet commitments through August 2, 2011.[19]

On Friday, May 6, the issuance of State and Local Government Series (SLGS) Treasury securities was suspended until further notice.[20] On May 16, 2011, Secretary Geithner notified Congress of his determination of a debt issuance suspension period and informed them of his intent to utilize extraordinary measures to create additional room under the debt ceiling to allow Treasury to continue funding the operations of the government.[21] Between May 16, 2011, and August 2, 2011, Treasury prematurely redeemed securities of the Civil Service Retirement and Disability Trust Fund and did not invest receipts of the Civil Service Retirement and Disability Trust Fund and the Postal Service Retiree Health Benefit Fund. Treasury also suspended investments in the Exchange Stabilization Fund and the Government Securities Investment Fund (G-Fund) of the Federal Thrift Savings Plan. Because these funds are required by law to be made whole once the debt limit is increased, these specific actions did not affect federal retirees or employees once the debt limit was increased.[22]

The debt limit was permanently increased on August 2, 2011, as part of the Budget Control Act of 2011 (BCA; P.L. 112-25), from $14,294 billion to $14,694 billion. The BCA provided for two additional debt limit increases. After the initial increase on August 2, 2011, the debt limit was permanently increased again on September 21, 2011, from $14,694 billion to $15,194 billion and again on January 27, 2012, from $15,194 billion to $16,394 billion.[23]

Actions in 2013

On December 26, 2012, Secretary Geithner sent a letter to Congress stating that the debt limit, the last increase provided for under the BCA, would be reached on December 31, 2012. Treasury estimated that the use of extraordinary measures would provide additional headroom under the debt limit until early 2013.[24] A debt issuance suspension period was declared on December 31, 2012, at which time Treasury prematurely redeemed securities of the Civil Service Retirement and Disability Trust Fund and did not invest receipts of the Civil Service Retirement and Disability Trust Fund and the Postal Service Retiree Health Benefit Fund.[25] On January 15, 2013, Secretary Geithner notified Congress that Treasury would suspend investments in the Government Securities Investment Fund (G-Fund) of the Federal Thrift Savings Plan.[26] On February 4, 2013, the statutory debt limit was suspended through May 18, 2013, as part of the No Budget, No Pay Act of 2013 (P.L. 113-3).

On May 19, 2013, the debt limit was reinstated and raised to $16,699 billion, a level which accommodated borrowing incurred during the suspension period.[27] The issuance of SLGS Treasury securities was suspended until further notice on May 15, 2013. A debt issuance suspension period was declared on May 20, 2013, at which time Treasury prematurely redeemed securities of the Civil Service Retirement and Disability Trust Fund and did not invest receipts of the Civil Service Retirement and Disability Trust Fund and the Postal Service Retiree Health Benefit Fund.[28] On May 31, 2013, Secretary Lew notified Congress that Treasury would suspend investments in the Government Securities Investment Fund (G-Fund) of the Federal Thrift Savings Plan.[29] On October 1, 2013, Treasury estimated that the extraordinary measures would be exhausted "no later than October 17, 2013."[30] On October 17, 2013, the debt limit was suspended through February 7, 2014, as part of the Continuing Appropriations Act, 2014 (P.L. 113-46).

Actions in 2014

On February 7, 2014, Secretary Lew sent a letter to Congress stating that at the end of the debt limit suspension period, Treasury would begin utilizing the extraordinary measures to finance government operations. Treasury estimated that the use of these extraordinary measures would provide additional headroom under the debt limit until February 27, 2014.[31] On February 10, 2014 (the next business day after the suspension period ended), the debt limit was reinstated and raised to $17,212 billion, a level which accommodated borrowing incurred during the suspension period. A debt issuance suspension period was declared on February 10, 2014, at which time Treasury prematurely redeemed securities of the Civil Service Retirement and Disability Trust Fund and suspended investments in the Government Securities Investment Fund (G-Fund) of the Federal Thrift Savings Plan.[32] On February 15, 2014, the debt limit was suspended for a third time through March 15, 2015, as part of the Temporary Debt Limit Extension Act (P.L. 113-83).

Actions in 2015

On March 13, 2015, Secretary Lew sent a letter to Congress stating that at the end of the debt limit suspension period, Treasury would begin using the extraordinary measures to finance government operations.[33] On March 16, 2015, the debt limit was reinstated and raised to $18,113 billion, a level which accommodated borrowing incurred during the suspension period. A debt issuance suspension period was declared on March 16, 2015, at which time Treasury prematurely redeemed securities and suspended investment of the Civil Service Retirement and Disability Trust Fund and Postal Service Retiree Health Benefits Fund and suspended investments in the Government Securities Investment Fund (G-Fund) of the Federal Thrift Savings Plan.[34] The Congressional Budget Office recently estimated the extraordinary measures would be exhausted around October or November 2015.[35]

Observations from Past Actions

As discussed above, short delays in increasing the debt limit have caused the Treasury Secretary to take extraordinary actions to avoid disrupting the payments of federal obligations. Though the federal government incurred additional costs during these periods, such as disruption of government borrowing and trust fund investment programs, the payment of benefits and other outlays occurred largely on schedule and trust funds were made whole once these crises ended.36 As long as the budget continues to be in deficit and policy makers wish to avoid a default on federal obligations, methods such as those described above cannot circumvent the need to eventually raise the debt limit.

POTENTIAL IMPLICATIONS OF REACHING AND NOT RAISING THE DEBT LIMIT

If the federal government were to reach the debt limit and Treasury were to exhaust its alternative strategies for remaining under the debt limit, then the federal government would need to rely solely on incoming revenues to finance obligations. If this occurred during a period when the federal government was running a deficit, the dollar amount of newly incurred federal obligations would continually exceed the dollar amount of newly incoming revenues.

It is not possible for CRS to specifically predict what Congress, the President, the Office of Management and Budget (OMB), Treasury, federal agencies, and financial markets would do in certain situations. Nevertheless, it is possible to scope out some aspects of what *could* happen under a specific scenario, in which the federal government is no longer able to issue debt, has exhausted alternative sources of cash, and therefore is dependent upon incoming receipts or other sources of funds to provide any cash that is necessary to pay federal obligations. That said, CRS cannot state the full range of events that may occur if the described scenario were to actually take place.

In this scenario, the federal government implicitly would be required to use some sort of decision-making rule about whether to pay obligations in the order they are received, or, alternatively, to prioritize which obligations to pay, while other obligations would go into an unpaid queue. In other words, the federal government's inability to borrow or use other means of financing implies that payment of some or all bills or obligations would be delayed.

Possible Options for Treasury: Could Prioritization Be Used?

Some have argued that prioritization of payments can be used by Treasury to avoid a default on selected federal obligations by paying interest on outstanding debt before other obligations.[37] Treasury officials have maintained that the department lacks formal legal authority to establish priorities to pay obligations, asserting, in effect, that each law obligating funds and authorizing expenditures stands on an equal footing.[38] In other words, Treasury would have to make payments on obligations as they come due.

In contrast to this view, GAO wrote to then-Chairman Bob Packwood of the Senate Finance Committee in 1985 that it was aware of no requirement that Treasury must pay outstanding obligations in the order in which they are received.[39] GAO concluded that "Treasury is free to liquidate obligations in any order it finds will best serve the interests of the United States." In any case, if Treasury were to prioritize, it is not clear what the priorities might be among the different types of spending.[40]

While the positions of Treasury and GAO may appear at first glance to differ, closer analysis suggests that they merely offer two different interpretations of silence in statute with respect to a prioritization system for paying obligations. On one hand, GAO's 1985 opinion posits that silence in statute with regard to prioritization simply leaves the determination of payment prioritization to the discretion of the Treasury Department. Conversely, Treasury appears to assert that the lack of specific statutory direction operates as a legal barrier, effectively preventing it from establishing a prioritization system.

Subsequently, Treasury noted in 2011 that an attempt to prioritize payments was "unworkable" because adopting a policy that would require certain types of payments taking precedence over other U.S. legal obligations would merely be "a failure by the U.S. to stand behind its commitments."[41] In an August 2012 letter, the Treasury Inspector General also addressed this topic by stating, "Treasury officials determined that there is no fair or sensible way to pick and choose among the many bills that come due every day. Furthermore, because Congress has never provided guidance to the contrary, Treasury's systems are designed to make each payment in the order it comes due."[42] At a hearing before the Senate Finance Committee in October 2013, Treasury Secretary Lew stated the following:

> We write roughly 80 million checks a month. The systems are automated to pay because for 224 years, the policy of Congress and every

president has been we pay our bills. You cannot go into those systems and easily make them pay some things and not other things. They weren't designed that way because it was never the policy of this government to be in the position that we would have to be in if we couldn't pay all our bills.[43]

Treasury offered additional information regarding its position on prioritization in May 2014 in response to questions posed by Representative Jeb Hensarling, chairman of the House Financial Services Committee. At that time, Treasury Assistant Secretary Fitzpayne stated that if the debt limit was reached and not raised and sufficient cash was available, the Federal Reserve Bank of New York would be technologically capable of continuing to make principal and interest payments on the debt. However, in this circumstance, Treasury would not be able to make payments on all other obligations. Assistant Secretary Fitzpayne warned that "this approach would be entirely experimental and create unacceptable risk to both domestic and global financial markets."[44]

Another perspective on prioritization relates to the Impoundment Control Act of 1974 (ICA), as amended.[45] The term *impoundment* refers to actions by the President, OMB, an agency head, or any officer or employee to preclude obligation or expenditure of budget authority. One type of impoundment action, *deferral*, refers to a temporary withholding or delaying of the obligation or expenditure of budget authority provided for projects or activities, or any other type of executive action or inaction which effectively precludes the obligation or expenditure of budget authority. Through the establishment of several statutory processes and restrictions, the ICA generally prohibited the use of discretion to effect "policy" impoundments. A policy impoundment might be, for example, a decision not to spend funds appropriated by Congress because a given federal activity may not be favored by a sitting President or agency official. Funds may be deferred only for certain reasons specified in 2 U.S.C. 684(b) (e.g., contingencies).[46] The relationship between prioritization associated with a debt limit impasse, on one hand, and the ICA, on the other, is that prioritization could be characterized as undertaking some spending but, due to lack of cash, deferring other spending.

In the event of a debt limit impasse, however, if the prioritization appears to disfavor certain programs, issues similar to those that gave rise to the ICA might resurface. These issues could include the balance of power between Congress and the President over spending priorities and the potential for use of prioritization in ways that Congress might not intend.[47] For example, if spending for a program that uses one-year funds were deferred until the end of a fiscal year, when the underlying budget authority expires, the deferral might constitute a functional equivalent of a rescission (cancellation of budget authority), akin to a line-item veto.[48] It appears that OMB and the Department of Justice have grappled with some of these issues in the past without coming to firm resolution, as evidenced by a 1995 internal OMB memorandum that was publicly released with papers of former White House Associate Counsel and current Supreme Court Justice Elena Kagan.[49]

Possible Options for OMB: Could Apportionment Be Used?

It also is possible that OMB may use statutory authority to apportion or reapportion budget authority (i.e., the authority to incur obligations) that Congress has granted in appropriations, contract, and borrowing authority to delay expenditures and effectively establish priorities for liquidating obligations. OMB is required by statute to "apportion" these funds (e.g., quarterly) to prevent agencies from spending at a rate that would exhaust their appropriations before the end of the fiscal year.[50] If OMB were to use statutory apportionment authority to affect the rate of federal spending, its ability to do so would be constrained by the Impoundment Control Act of 1974, as amended.[51] As noted earlier, the Impoundment Control Act does not prohibit the President from withholding funds, but establishes procedures for the President to submit formal requests to Congress either to defer (i.e., delay) spending until later or to rescind (i.e., cancel) the budget authority that Congress previously had granted.[52] Although the use of OMB's apportionment authority in the event of a debt limit crisis might delay the need to pay some obligations, use of the authority would not prevent obligations from remaining unpaid.

Potential Impacts on Government Operations

If the debt limit is reached and not increased, federal spending would be affected. Under normal circumstances, Treasury has sufficient financial resources to liquidate all obligations arising from discretionary and mandatory (direct) spending, the latter of which includes interest payments on the debt.[53] If a lapse in raising the debt limit should prevent Treasury from being able to liquidate all obligations on time, it is not clear whether the distinction between different types of spending would be significant or whether the need to establish priorities would disproportionately impact one type of spending or another. It is also not clear whether the distinctions among different types of obligations, such as contract, grant, benefit, and interest payments, would prove to be significant.

Potential Impacts on Programs Generally

A government that delays paying its obligations in effect borrows from vendors, contractors, beneficiaries, other governments,[54] or employees who are not paid on time. Moreover, a backlog of unpaid bills would continue to grow until the government collects more revenues or other sources of cash than its outlays. In some cases, delaying federal payments incurs interest penalties under some statutes such as the Prompt Payment Act, which directs the government to pay interest penalties to contractors if it does not pay them by the required payment date,[55] and the Internal Revenue Code, which requires the government to pay interest penalties if tax refunds are delayed beyond a certain date.[56] The specific impacts of delayed payment would depend upon the nature of the federal program or activity for which funds are to be paid.

Potential Impacts on Programs with Trust Funds

If Treasury delays investing a federal trust fund's revenues in government securities, or redeems prematurely a federal trust fund's holdings of government securities, the result would be a loss of interest to the affected trust fund. This could potentially worsen the financial situation of the affected trust fund(s) and accelerate insolvency dates.57 As noted earlier, Congress passed P.L. 104-121 to prevent federal officials from using the Social Security and Medicare Trust Funds for debt management purposes, except when necessary to provide for the payment of benefits and administrative expenses of the programs. Under P.L. 99-509, Treasury is permitted to delay investment in the TSP's G-Fund and the Civil Service Retirement and Disability Trust Fund, and also to redeem prematurely assets of the Civil Service Retirement and Disability Trust Fund. However, the law also requires Treasury to make these funds whole after a debt limit impasse is resolved. The government maintains a number of other trust funds whose finances could potentially be harmed by delayed investment or early redemption in the absence of similar actions to make the trust funds whole after a debt limit impasse has ended.

Distinction between a Debt Limit Crisis and a Government Shutdown

In 1995, the Congressional Budget Office contrasted this sort of scenario, under which the debt limit is reached and not raised, with a substantially different situation, in which the government must shut down due to lack of appropriations.

> Failing to raise the debt ceiling would not bring the government to a screeching halt the way that not passing appropriations bills would. Employees would not be sent home, and checks would continue to be issued. If the Treasury was low on cash, however, there could be delays in honoring checks and disruptions in the normal flow of government services.[58]

Alternatively stated, in a situation when the debt limit is reached and Treasury exhausts its financing alternatives, aside from ongoing cash flow, an agency may continue to obligate funds. However, Treasury may not be able to liquidate all obligations that result in federal outlays due to a shortage of cash. In contrast to this, if Congress and the President do not enact interim or full-year appropriations for an agency, the agency does not have budget authority available for obligation. If this occurs, the agency must shut down non-excepted activities, with immediate effects on government services.[59]

Potential Economic and Financial Effects

In addition to the potential impact on federal programs and activities if the debt limit is not increased, there may also be economic and financial consequences. A 1979 GAO report described the consequences of failing to increase the debt ceiling. GAO said the government had never defaulted on any of its securities, because cash has been available to pay interest and redeem them upon maturity or demand.[60] Further, GAO said a default on the securities could have adverse effects on the economy, the public welfare, and the government's ability to market future securities.

> It is difficult to perceive all the adverse effects that a government default for even a short time would have on the economy and the public welfare. It is generally recognized that a default would preclude the government from honoring all of its obligations to pay for such things as employees' salaries and wages; social security benefits, civil service

retirement, and other benefits from trust funds; contractual services and supplies, and maturing securities.... At a minimum, however, the government could be subject to additional claims for interest on unredeemed matured debt and to claims for damages resulting from failure to make payments. But even beyond that, the full faith and credit of the U.S. government would be threatened. Domestic money markets, in which government securities play a major role, could be affected substantially.[61]

If the debt limit were reached and interest payments on debt were paid, it is not clear what the repercussions would be on the financial markets or the economy. If Treasury had to rely on incoming cash to pay its obligations, a significant portion of government spending would go unpaid. Removing a portion of government spending from the economy would leave behind significant economic effects and would have an effect on gross domestic product (GDP) by definition, all other things being equal.[62] Further, if the government fails to make timely payments to individuals, service providers, and other organizations, these persons and entities would also be affected. Even if the government continued paying interest, it is not clear whether creditors would retain or lose faith in the government's willingness to pay its obligations. If creditors lost this confidence, the federal government's interest costs would likely increase substantially and there would likely be broader disruptions to financial markets.

On April 25, 2011, the Treasury Borrowing Advisory Committee[63] sent a letter to Secretary Geithner expressing its views on the impact on financial markets if the debt ceiling is not raised.[64] The letter warned that any delay by Treasury in making an interest or principal payment could trigger "another catastrophic financial crisis." Further, the committee described several potential consequences stemming from a Treasury default on its obligations including a downgrade of the U.S. credit rating, an increase in federal and private borrowing costs, damage to the economic recovery, and broader disruptions to the financial system. Finally, the committee also warned that a prolonged delay in raising the debt limit could have negative consequences on the market before the time when default would actually occur.[65]

Effects of 2011 and 2013 "Brinkmanship"[66]

Extended debate over whether or not to raise the debt limit can also have financial and economic consequences even if the debt limit does eventually get raised. While not causing financial instability, what has been referred to as "brinkmanship" can lead to worse economic or financial outcomes than raising the debt limit well ahead of time. While the debt limit impasse has no direct effect on the economy because it does not interfere with government financing, it could still have had indirect effects on GDP and financial conditions if it altered the behavior of households and businesses.

The effects of "brinkmanship" can be answered by observing what happened to the economy and financial markets during the 2011 and 2013 debt limit impasse. Neither episode caused financial disruption or recession. In 2013, growth was strong in the fourth quarter when the impasse occurred, but declined in the following quarter.[67] Nevertheless, both episodes had discernible effects. Economic growth in the third quarter of 2011 was noticeably slower (1.4%) than the preceding or following quarter, although it is difficult to isolate how much of that slowdown could be attributed to the debt limit impasse.[68] The Treasury Department released a report detailing how the August 2011 debt limit impasse coincided with a marked decline in consumer confidence, small business optimism, and the S&P 500 stock index, and an increase in the equity market volatility index ("VIX"). In each case, these indicators did not return to their previous levels until several months after the debt limit was raised.[69] The Treasury report does not attempt to isolate the effects of the debt limit impasse from other events that would also affect financial markets concurrently. Notably, the debt limit impasse also resulted in the first downgrade of federal debt by a major credit rating agency, when Standard & Poor's downgraded the debt from AAA on August 5, 2011. In its statement on the downgrade, S&P said that

> More broadly, the downgrade reflects our view that the effectiveness, stability, and predictability of American policymaking and political institutions have weakened at a time of ongoing fiscal and economic challenges to a degree more than we envisioned ... [70]

Thus, as their statement would suggest, another channel through which the debt limit might affect private spending is via heightened policy uncertainty.

By contrast, however, those same indicators showed a much smaller deterioration in October 2013. Consumer confidence also fell in October 2013, although this may have been partly caused by the concurrent government shutdown. It remained at higher levels than in August 2011 or during the financial crisis, however. The S&P 500 stock index fell by less than 3% during the shutdown, but had recovered its previous value by the time the government was reopened.

This suggests that either investors felt more confident that the debt limit would ultimately be raised (perhaps because it had been raised in similar circumstances in 2011) or other factors, such as the downgrade, are responsible for the greater deterioration in credit markets in August 2011.[71]

The two financial instruments that experienced the most pronounced price movements in the 2011 and 2013 debt limit impasses were short-term Treasury securities and credit default swaps (CDS) on U.S. Treasuries. First, Treasury yields exhibited a highly unusual pattern. For example, from October 1 to October 16, 2013, yields on Treasury bills maturing in four weeks exceeded those maturing in three months. The consensus explanation for this phenomenon was fear that a failure to raise the debt limit in a timely fashion could cause short-term interruptions in repaying maturing debt, and the unusual pattern disappeared as soon as the debt limit was raised. (The rest of the yield curve has not exhibited any unusual movements recently.) Nevertheless, the yield on 4-week bills (0.32% on October 15) implied that this risk was still perceived to be relatively low. Since noticeably higher rates were not manifested throughout the rest of the Treasury yield curve, the broader economic consequences of this anomaly were likely limited. Their main effect was to directly raise the borrowing costs of the Treasury on securities sold during the period of elevated yields. In the 2011 debt limit impasse, GAO estimated that the debt limit impasse increased Treasury borrowing costs by $1.3 billion in 2011.[72]

Second, CDS prices for which Treasury securities are the reference entity rose significantly. Credit default swaps for which federal debt is the reference entity would trigger a payment from the seller of the CDS to the buyer if the security experiences a "credit event" related to timely and full payment.[73] In 2011, CDS prices for five-year Treasury securities (i.e., the cost to insure against default) rose above 60 basis points, for example; this level was unusually high compared with historical standards, but lower than at the depth of the 2008 financial crisis.[74] At its peak on October 10, 2013, CDS prices for five-year Treasury securities more than doubled compared to the previous month, rising to 40 basis points; this price was below the peak price in 2011.[75]

It is difficult to disentangle the effects of the debt limit impasse from the effects of the government shutdown, which happened simultaneously.

CONSIDERATIONS FOR THE CURRENT DEBT LIMIT DEBATE

There are various viewpoints about how to deal with debt limit issues. The debt subject to limit will generally continue to rise as long as the budget remains in deficit and/or trust funds remain in surplus. To avoid raising the debt limit and continue normal government operations, significant spending cuts and/or revenue increases would be required.

Views on the Debt Limit, Prioritization, and Default

Members of the Obama Administration have maintained that not raising the debt limit would cause serious consequences. Former Treasury Secretary Geithner repeatedly asserted that not increasing the debt limit and, therefore, not meeting the country's obligations as a result "would cause irreparable harm to the American economy and to the livelihoods of all Americans."[76] President Obama has also repeatedly stated that the debt limit must be raised and he will not negotiate on this issue. He stated, "The financial well-being of the American people is not leverage to be used. The full faith and credit of the United States of America is not a bargaining chip."[77]

Speaker of the House John A. Boehner has stated that the debt limit should not be increased without "spending cuts or reforms" greater than the amount of the increase.[78] Senate Majority Leader Harry Reid has stated that he will require a balanced approach to dealing with the budget deficit and the debt with spending cuts paired with "revenue measures asking millionaires to pay their fair share." In the absence of an agreement to this effect, he remains committed to the spending cuts already in place.[79]

Economists have expressed concern regarding the current level of federal debt. However, they generally maintain that there would be significant consequences if the debt limit is not raised. Federal Reserve Chairman Ben Bernanke has stated that Congress must work to put a plan in to place that would lower the nation's federal debt. He also stated that not raising the debt limit could ultimately lead the nation to default on its debt with catastrophic implications for the financial system and the economy.[80] Mark Zandi, chief economist for Moody's Analytics, expressed similar sentiments regarding the debt limit and the potential impact on the economy. He stated, "Global investors are already anxious regarding our ability to come to a political consensus to address the nation's fiscal challenges; a protracted debate over the debt ceiling would be very counterproductive."[81] Donald Marron, the former director of the Urban-Brookings Tax Policy Center and a former Acting Director of the Congressional Budget Office, expressed similar views in January 2011. He stated, "Geithner is correct that the debt limit must increase. With monthly deficits running more than $100 billion, it's simply unthinkable that Congress could cut spending or increase revenue enough to avoid borrowing more.... Still, I am troubled by any suggestion that the United States might willingly default on its public debt. Doing so would have absolutely no upside."[82]

Questions have been raised regarding what constitutes a legal "default" by the government. Some proponents of a prioritization system suggest that the term "default" applies only if the government fails to pay interest on debt obligations held by third parties. Opponents of prioritization appear to argue that the term "default" applies not only to a failure to pay third-party debt holders, but also to the failure by the government to meet any obligation authorized by law, which would include a failure to fund an appropriated program, pay federal salaries or benefits, or pay an amount owed on a federal contract. No general statutory definition of the term "default" exists; however, *Black's Law Dictionary* 428 (7th Ed. 1999) defines the term "default" as "the failure to make a payment when due," which, if accepted as the governing definition, would not appear to distinguish between various types of government obligations.

Aside from technical definitions, financial markets' perceptions of what constitutes a default, or a real threat of default, may be more relevant when assessing the potential impacts of not raising the debt limit. For example, if the federal government were to prioritize payments on debt obligations above other obligations, it is not clear whether financial markets would find this distinction to be significant when deciding whether and how to invest in federal government Treasury securities, since Treasury would be postponing payments on other legal obligations. Because perceptions such as these are difficult if not impossible to predict, it is not clear what the effects of prioritization would be, in the event of an impasse.[83] In the event of reaching the debt limit and the enactment of prioritization legislation, certain payments would receive priority. However, issues also might arise related to how a President, OMB, or an agency prioritizes among any obligations and expenditures that are not explicitly subject to prioritization, by statute. As noted earlier in this report, circumstances like these could prompt issues similar to those that gave rise to the Impoundment Control Act of 1974.

Legislative Action in the 113ᵗʰ Congress[84]

On April 30, 2013, the House Ways and Means Committee reported the Full Faith and Credit Act (H.R. 807, 113ᵗʰ Congress). This legislation, as reported by the committee, would require Treasury to prioritize payments on obligations of debt held by the public and to the Social Security Trust Funds in the event that the debt limit is reached and to provide weekly reports of these obligations. On May 9, 2013, the House approved this legislation by a vote of 221-207. A similar measure was included as part of proposed legislation to provide for appropriations for a portion of FY2014 via a continuing resolution. The legislation, including this provision, was approved by the House on September 20, 2013 (H.J.Res. 59, 113ᵗʰ Congress) though ultimately not included in the final bill enacted into law.

Can an Increase in the Current Debt Limit Be Avoided?

Budget outlays and revenue collections over the fiscal year, along with the funds contained in the extraordinary measures, will affect the timing of the debate over raising the debt limit. On March 16, 2015, the debt limit was reset to $18,113 billion. Under current estimates, debt levels will reach $18,473 billion or $360 billion above the current limit by the end of FY2015 under current law.[85] If the extraordinary measures are exhausted, Treasury will no longer be able to issue federal debt absent further legislative action. At that time, federal spending would have to be decreased or federal revenues would have to be increased by a corresponding amount to cover what cannot be borrowed. If Congress and the President enact legislation raising future levels of spending or lowering revenues without providing offsets, the borrowing needs of government would increase as the deficit grows larger.

How Much Should the Debt Limit Be Raised?

Despite recent declines in the budget deficit, several current policy proposals project increases in the debt subject to limit over the next 10 years. Under President Obama's FY2016 budget, the debt subject to limit is projected to reach $26,242 billion at the end of FY2025.[86] This represents an increase of roughly $770 billion, on average, in each fiscal year during the FY2016 to FY2025 period. Increases in debt subject to limit at this level occur even as the budget deficit is projected to decline, in nominal dollars, between FY2015 and

FY2017. Between FY2018 and FY2020, the budget deficit is projected to remain roughly stable, though at slightly higher levels than the previous period.[87] In other words, the debt subject to limit increases even if the budget deficit declines in nominal terms as issuing debt would still be required to finance the projected federal spending in excess of federal revenues.

According to the figures provided in the House Budget Committee report (H.Rept. 114-47) accompanying the House FY2016 Budget Resolution (H.Con.Res. 27, 114th Congress) agreed to on March 25, 2015, the debt subject to limit is projected to rise from $19,048 billion at the end of FY2016 to $20,905 billion at the end of FY2025. This means that, if the policies contained in the House-passed budget resolution were to be enacted, the debt limit would have to increase by $1,857 billion (or roughly $200 billion in each fiscal year) during the FY2016 to FY2025 period to accommodate these proposals.[88]

Given the borrowing requirements under both the President's FY2016 budget and the House-passed budget resolution, the current estimates stipulate the increases in the debt limit that would be required. However, depending on the spending and revenue proposals that may be enacted, borrowing requirements could change going forward. These borrowing requirements will dictate the level of debt and future increases in the debt limit. How often Congress wishes to reconsider statutory debt limit legislation typically affects the level at which the debt limit is set.

Temporary increases in the debt limit have been used in the past to provide additional time for Congress to consider debt limit increases. However, past temporary debt limit increases were eventually followed by permanent increases. If a temporary increase were to expire and the debt limit were to revert to a prior lower level, Congress may want to enact legislation that would result in a budget surplus in excess of the intragovernmental surplus in order to lower the level of debt subject to limit. If this legislation is not enacted and fully realized prior to the expiration of the temporary limit, then the level of debt would exceed the lowered debt limit.

IMPLICATIONS OF FUTURE FEDERAL DEBT ON THE DEBT LIMIT

It is extremely difficult for Congress to effectively influence short-term fiscal and budgetary policy through action on legislation adjusting the debt limit. For example, the debt could reach the statutory limit after spending and revenue decisions for the current fiscal year have already been made. The need to raise (or lower) the limit during a session of Congress is driven by previous decisions regarding revenues and spending. These decisions stem from legislation enacted earlier in the session or in prior years.

From the Congressional Budget Office:

> By itself, setting a limit on the debt is an ineffective means of controlling deficits because the decisions that necessitate borrowing are made through other legislative actions. By the time an increase in the debt ceiling comes up for approval, it is too late to avoid paying the government's pending bills without incurring serious negative consequences.[89]

Nevertheless, the consideration of debt limit legislation often is viewed as an opportunity to reexamine fiscal and budgetary policy. Consequently, House and Senate action on legislation adjusting the debt limit often is complicated, hindered by policy disagreements, and subject to delay.[90] Many in Congress have stated that the debt limit should not be raised without accompanying deficit reduction legislation.

Generally, the following scenarios dictate whether or not an increase in the debt limit would be necessary, all else constant:

- If the federal budget is in deficit and intragovernmental debt is rising, an increase in the debt limit would be necessary.
- If the federal budget is in deficit and intragovernmental debt falls by an amount that is smaller than the budget deficit, an increase in the debt limit would be necessary.
- If the federal budget is balanced or in surplus and intragovernmental debt rises by an amount that is larger than the budget surplus, an increase in the debt limit would be necessary.
- If the federal budget is balanced or in surplus and intragovernmental debt is falling, an increase in the debt limit would not be required.

In other words, increases in the statutory debt limit would be required if the budget remains in deficit, even if future deficit levels are lower than they are at present, or if there are increases in the level of intragovernmental debt. If intragovernmental debt is declining, presumably due to the need of certain trust funds to redeem their holdings of Treasury securities in order to pay benefits, Treasury would have to provide the trust funds with cash either from the General Fund resources or by issuing additional debt to the public to raise cash. If the federal budget is in deficit, Treasury would have to raise the necessary cash to redeem trust fund securities by issuing debt to the public. This would not require an increase in the debt limit, as the decline in intragovernmental debt would be offset by an equal increase in debt held by the public. A decline in intragovernmental debt as a result of a redemption in trust fund securities could be financed by using surplus cash if the federal budget is in surplus at that time.[91] In this situation, debt held by the public, debt held by government accounts, and total federal debt would decrease. If the budget surplus were less than the reduction in intragovernmental debt, the increase in the debt held by the public would be offset by the decline in intragovernmental debt, resulting in a decrease in the total debt.

APPENDIX. DETAILED HISTORY ON PAST TREASURY ACTIONS DURING PREVIOUS DEBT LIMIT CRISES

Selected Actions in 1985

In September 1985, the Treasury Department informed Congress that it had reached the statutory debt limit. As a result, Treasury had to take extraordinary measures to meet the government's cash requirements. Treasury used various internal transactions involving the Federal Financing Bank (FFB) and delayed public auctions of government debt. It also was unable to issue, or had to delay issuing, new short-term government securities to the Civil Service Retirement and Disability Trust Fund, the Social Security Trust Funds, and several smaller trust funds. Issuing new government securities to the trust funds would have caused the federal debt to exceed the debt limit. During this period, the bulk of Social Security payroll tax revenues were kept in a non-interest bearing account.

Treasury took the additional step of "disinvesting" the Civil Service Retirement and Disability Trust Fund, the Social Security Trust Funds, and several smaller trust funds by redeeming some trust fund securities earlier than usual. Premature redemption of these securities created room under the debt ceiling for Treasury to borrow sufficient cash from the public to pay other obligations, including November Social Security benefits.[92]

As a result of these various actions, Social Security benefit payments and other federal payments were not jeopardized. The debt limit was subsequently temporarily increased on November 14, 1985 (P.L. 99-155), and permanently increased on December 12, 1985 (P.L. 99-177), from $1,824 billion to $2,079 billion. Both P.L. 99-155 and P.L. 99-177 included provisions to require Treasury to restore any interest income lost to the trust funds as a result of delayed investments and early redemptions.

Concerning Treasury's management of the Social Security Trust Funds during the 1985 debt limit impasse, the General Accounting Office (GAO, now the Government Accountability Office) wrote: "We conclude that, although some of the Secretary's actions appear in retrospect to have been in violation of the requirements of the Social Security Act, we cannot say that the Secretary acted unreasonably given the extraordinary situation in which he was operating."[93] In particular, GAO found that not all the delayed investment and securities redemptions during the period from September through November 1985 were necessary to meet Social Security benefit payments, and the excess was used to finance general government operations.[94]

Following the 1985 debt limit crisis, Congress formally authorized the Secretary of the Treasury to declare a debt issuance suspension period and, during such periods, to depart from normal trust fund investment practices with respect to certain funds such as the Civil Service Retirement and Disability Fund and the TSP's G Fund (P.L. 99-509, the Omnibus Budget Reconciliation Act of 1986). Funds raised by procedures authorized during a debt issuance suspension period can only be used to the extent necessary to prevent the public debt from exceeding the debt limit. After the debt issuance suspension period has ended, P.L. 99-509 requires Treasury to make the trust funds whole by issuing the appropriate amount of securities and crediting any interest lost due to non-investment or early disinvestment of these funds.[95] Such authority to depart from normal trust fund investment practices was not provided with respect to the Social Security Trust Funds. A provision to allow such authority was dropped from P.L. 99-509 during conference.

Selected Actions in 1995-1996

Following the enactment of this additional authority, the first debt issuance suspension period was announced on November 15, 1995. Treasury, once again, used non-traditional methods of financing, including some of the methods used during the 1985 crisis as well as not reinvesting some of the maturing Treasury securities held by the Exchange Stabilization Fund.[96] In addition, Treasury utilized the new authority that was enacted under P.L. 99-509 to declare a debt issuance suspension period.

In early 1996, Treasury announced that it had insufficient cash to pay Social Security benefits for March 1996.[97] Congress responded on February 1, 1996, by passing P.L. 104-103, which provided Treasury with temporary authority to issue securities to the public in an amount equal to the March 1996 Social Security benefit payments. Treasury issued about $29 billion of securities on February 23, 1996, and, under P.L. 104-103, these new securities were not to count against the debt limit until March 15, 1996. On March 7, 1996, Congress passed P.L. 104-115, which amended P.L. 104-103 to permit Treasury to continue investing payroll tax revenues in government securities and also to extend the exemption of the securities issued under P.L. 104-103 from counting against the debt limit until March 30, 1996.

The debt limit was permanently increased on March 29, 1996 (P.L. 104-121) from $4,900 billion to $5,500 billion. P.L. 104-121 also codified Congress's understanding that the Secretary of the Treasury and other federal officials are not authorized to use Social Security and Medicare funds for debt management purposes.[98] SSA states the following:

> Specifically, the Secretary of the Treasury and other federal officials are required not to delay or otherwise underinvest incoming receipts to the Social Security and Medicare Trust Funds. They are also required not to sell, redeem, or otherwise disinvest securities, obligations, or other assets of these Trust Funds except when necessary to provide for the payment of benefits and administrative expenses of the programs.[99]

These restrictions apply to the Federal Old-Age and Survivors Insurance (OASI) Trust Fund, the Federal Disability Insurance (DI) Trust Fund, the Federal Hospital Insurance (HI) Trust Fund, and the Federal Supplementary Medical Insurance (SMI) Trust Fund.

Selected Actions in 2011

Beginning in January 2011, Treasury again took actions to avoid reaching the debt limit and began notifying Congress of its intentions. On January 6, 2011, Treasury Secretary Geithner sent a letter to Congress stating that Treasury had the ability to delay the date by which the debt limit would be reached by utilizing similar methods used during past crises, including declaring a debt issuance suspension period, if necessary. According to Treasury, these actions could delay the date that the debt limit would be reached by several weeks. However, if the debt limit was not raised after that point, payment of other obligations and benefits would be "discontinued, limited, or adversely affected."[100]

On April 4, 2011, Secretary Geithner issued another letter to Congress stating that the debt limit would be reached no later than May 16, 2011, and the use of extraordinary measures would extend Treasury's ability to meet commitments through July 8, 2011. Beyond these extraordinary measures discussed in the letter and detailed earlier, Treasury stated that it did not have other actions available that year that it could take to find additional authority to issue debt. The letter further stated that the sale of certain financial assets would not be a viable option to avoid increasing the debt limit.[101]

On May 2, 2011, Secretary Geithner issued a third letter to Congress reiterating that the debt limit would be reached no later than May 16, 2011, but that the use of extraordinary measures would extend Treasury's ability to meet commitments through August 2, 2011. The revision in the latter date was a result of stronger than expected tax receipts. Further, Secretary Geithner again stated that not raising the debt limit "would have catastrophic economic impact that would be felt by every American" and that federal payments would be affected.[102] In addition, the letter stated that on Friday, May 6, the issuance of State and Local Government Series (SLGS) Treasury securities would be suspended until further notice.[103]

On May 16, 2011, Secretary Geithner notified Congress of a debt issuance suspension period and informed them of his intent to utilize extraordinary measures to create additional room under the debt ceiling to allow Treasury to continue funding the operations of the government.[104] Between May 16, 2011, and August 2, 2011, Treasury prematurely redeemed securities of the Civil Service Retirement and Disability Trust Fund and did not invest receipts of the Civil Service Retirement and Disability Trust Fund and the Postal Service Retiree Health Benefit Fund. Treasury also suspended investments in the Exchange Stabilization Fund and the Government Securities Investment Fund (G-Fund) of the Federal Thrift Savings Plan. Because these funds are required by law to be made whole once the debt limit is increased, these specific actions did not affect federal retirees or employees once the debt limit was increased.[105] The debt limit was permanently increased on August 2, 2011 (Budget Control Act of 2011 or BCA; P.L. 112-25), from $14,294 billion to $14,694 billion.

The enactment of P.L. 112-25 provided for three separate debt limit increases. The first, as discussed above, permanently increased the debt limit on August 2, 2011. Thereafter, the debt limit was permanently increased on September 21, 2011, from $14,694 billion to $15,194 billion and on January 27, 2012, from $15,194 billion to $16,394 billion.[106] Secretary Geithner has stated that the current debt limit would be reached on December 31, 2012, and the use of extraordinary measures would provide additional headroom under the debt limit until early 2013.[107]

Views on the Debt Limit, Prioritization, and Default During the 2011 Debt Limit Debate

During the debate over the debt limit in 2011, both the Administration and Congress maintained various views on this issue. Members of the Obama Administration stated that default cannot be avoided if the debt limit is not raised, and that the consequences of a federal default would be serious. Treasury Secretary Geithner's letter of January 6, 2011, provided Treasury's views on the "consequences of default by the United States." The letter described, among other things, federal payments that would be "discontinued, limited, or adversely affected."[108] The letter also said a short-term or limited default on legal obligations would cause "catastrophic damage to the economy."[109] Chairman of the White House Council of Economic Advisers Austan Goolsbee elaborated, saying that a default would cause "a worse financial economic crisis than anything we saw in 2008."[110] Secretary Geithner, in his letter to Congress, added, "Default would have prolonged and far-reaching negative consequences on the safe-haven status of Treasuries and the dollar's dominant role in the international financial system, causing further increases in interest rates and reducing the willingness of investors here and around the world to invest in the United States."[111] In a later online posting, Treasury Deputy Secretary Neal Wolin wrote that proposals to prioritize payments on the national debt above other legal obligations would not prevent default and would bring the same economic consequences Secretary Geithner described.[112] Looking forward, Secretary Geithner said in his letter that in addition to addressing the debt limit, President Obama wanted to work with Congress to address the federal government's fiscal position with particular attention to addressing "medium- and long-term fiscal challenges."[113]

Other policy makers have expressed some contrasting perspectives focusing on the need to tie proposals to raise the debt limit to spending cuts, changes in the budget process, or instructions on how to deal with the payment of obligations if the debt limit is reached. For example, Senator Jim DeMint wrote in an op-ed that a vote to raise the debt limit should be opposed "unless Congress first passes a balanced-budget amendment that requires a two-thirds majority to raise taxes."[114]

Legislative proposals related to the potential debt limit crisis began emerging in early 2011. For example, Senator Pat Toomey and Representative Tom McClintock introduced legislation that, in the event of a debt limit crisis, would require Treasury to make payment of principal and interest on debt held by the public a higher priority than all other federal government obligations (S. 163/H.R. 421, 112th Congress). In a letter to Secretary Geithner, Senator Toomey said "This legislation is designed to maintain orderly financial markets by reassuring investors in U.S. Treasury securities that their investments are perfectly safe even in the unlikely event that the debt limit is temporarily reached."[115] Similarly, Senator David Vitter and Representative Dean Heller introduced legislation that would require priority be given to payment of all obligations on the debt held by the public and Social Security benefits in the event that the debt limit is reached (S. 259/H.R. 568, 112th Congress).[116] Representative Marlin Stutzman introduced legislation that would require priority be given to payment of all obligations on the debt held by the public, Social Security benefits, and specified military expenditures in the event that the debt limit is reached (H.R. 728, 112th Congress).[117] As noted earlier, Congress passed and the President signed the Budget Control Act, which addressed the debt limit and several aspects of fiscal policy.

Social Security Trust Fund Cash and Investment Management Practices

By law, the Social Security Trust Funds must be invested in interest-bearing obligations of the United States or in obligations guaranteed as to both principal and interest by the United States (42 U.S.C. §401(d) and 42 U.S.C. §1320b-15).[118] The securities that Treasury issues to the Social Security Trust Funds count toward the federal debt limit.

Under normal procedures, Social Security revenues (Social Security payroll taxes and individual income taxes) are immediately credited to the Social Security Trust Funds in the form of short-term, non-marketable Treasury securities called certificates of indebtedness (CIs). Under the terms of this exchange, when Treasury credits payroll tax and other revenues to Social Security in the form of CIs, the revenues themselves become available in the General Fund for other government operations.

CIs generally mature on the following June 30. Each June 30, any surplus for the year is converted from short-term Treasury securities to long-term, non-marketable Treasury securities called "special-issue obligations" or "specials."[119] In addition, other special issues that have just matured and that are not needed to pay near-term benefits are reinvested in special-issue obligations. Interest income is credited to the trust funds semi-annually (on June 30 and December 31) in the form of additional special-issue obligations.[120]

Social Security benefits are paid by Treasury from the General Fund. When Treasury pays Social Security benefits, it redeems an equivalent amount of Treasury securities held by the trust funds in order to reimburse the General Fund.

The Social Security program is projected to run a cash deficit through the 75-year forecast period. That is, Social Security's tax revenues are projected to be less than outlays for benefit payments and administration.[121] In a year when Social Security runs a cash flow deficit, Treasury redeems some long-term government securities held by the trust funds. However, Social Security will still need to invest in non-marketable, short-term government securities to manage short-term cash flows during the periods between receiving revenues and paying benefits (42 U.S.C. §401(a), 42 U.S.C. §401(d) and 42 U.S.C. §1320b-15). Investing the trust funds' revenues for even very short periods ensures that the trust funds maximize their interest earnings. Social Security will also need to invest in non-marketable, long-term government securities in June of each year, when short-term and certain long-term trust fund securities mature and amounts not needed to pay near-term benefits are rolled over into long-term government securities, and in June and December of each year, when semi-annual interest income is paid in the form of government securities.

In 2011 and 2012, Social Security drew on general revenues as a result of the Tax Relief, Unemployment Insurance Reauthorization, and Job Creation Act of 2010 (P.L. 111-312, as amended by P.L. 112-78 and P.L. 112-96). P.L. 111-312 provided a temporary 2 percentage point reduction in the Social Security payroll tax for employees and the self-employed in 2011, resulting in a tax rate of 4.2% for employees and 10.4% for the self-employed.[122] To protect the trust funds, P.L. 111-312 appropriated to the Social Security Trust Funds amounts equal to the reduction in payroll tax revenues. P.L. 111-312 specified that the appropriated amounts "shall be transferred from the General Fund at such times and in such manner as to replicate to the extent possible the transfers which would have occurred to such Trust Fund had such amendments not been enacted."[123] On December 23, 2011, Congress passed H.R. 3765 and

President Obama signed the bill into law as P.L. 112-78 to extend the payroll tax reduction for workers and the general revenue transfers through February 2012. On February 17, 2012, the House and the Senate agreed to the conference report on H.R. 3630, which further extended the payroll tax reduction for workers and the general revenue transfers through the end of calendar year 2012. H.R. 3630 was signed into law by President Obama on February 22, 2012 (P.L. 112-96).

Depending on the extent and duration of any future debt limit crisis, and also on Treasury prioritization decisions, Social Security Trust Fund investment management procedures and benefit payments potentially could be affected because of the requirement that Treasury obligations cannot be issued to the Social Security Trust Funds if doing so would exceed the debt limit.[124] At the same time, as described above, P.L. 104-121 restricts the Treasury Secretary's ability to delay or otherwise underinvest incoming receipts to the Social Security and Medicare Trust Funds. Delayed issuance of government obligations to the Trust Funds, or early redemption of some Trust Fund assets, could accelerate depletion of the Trust Funds and move up the expected insolvency date, absent congressional action to make the Trust Funds whole.

Depending on the government's cash position in a given month, Treasury may need to issue new public debt to raise the cash needed to pay benefits. Treasury may be unable to issue new public debt, however, if doing so would exceed the debt limit. Social Security benefit payments may be delayed or jeopardized if Treasury does not have enough cash on hand to pay benefits.

End Notes

[1] The current level of federal debt can be found in the U.S. Department of the Treasury, Daily Treasury Statement, Table III-C, available at http://fms.treas.gov/dts/index.html.

[2] The possible scenario sometimes has been referred to generically as a debt limit crisis. U.S. General Accounting Office (now the Government Accountability Office and hereinafter GAO), Debt Ceiling: Analysis of Actions During the 2003 Debt Issuance Suspension Periods, GAO-04-526, May 2004.

[3] This section draws on CRS Report 98-453, Debt-Limit Legislation in the Congressional Budget Process, by Bill Heniff Jr., and CRS Report RL31967, The Debt Limit: History and Recent Increases, by D. Andrew Austin and Mindy R. Levit.

[4] If the budget is in surplus and intragovernmental debt rises by an amount that is less than the budget surplus, the total debt would not increase. See the later discussion in the section titled "Implications of Future Federal Debt on the Debt Limit."

[5] GAO, Federal Trust and Other Earmarked Funds Answers to Frequently Asked Questions, GAO-01-199SP, January 2001, pp. 17-18.

[6] For an explanation of how this process works for the Social Security Trust Funds, see the section of the Appendix titled "Social Security Trust Fund Cash and Investment Management Practices."

[7] Chapter 56, 40 Stat. 288 (1917). The debt limit is now codified at 31 U.S.C. §3101.

[8] Treasury currently defines "Total Public Debt Subject to Limit" as "the Total Public Debt Outstanding less Unamortized Discount on Treasury Bills and Zero-Coupon Treasury Bonds, old debt issued prior to 1917, and old currency called United States Notes, as well as Debt held by the Federal Financing Bank and Guaranteed Debt." Approximately 0.1% of total federal debt is not subject to the debt limit. For more information, see U.S. Office of Management and Budget (hereinafter OMB), Budget of the U.S. Government for FY2014, Analytical Perspectives, Chapter 5 and Table 5-2.

[9] See generally, 31 U.S.C. §§3321 et seq. for the Treasury Secretary's duty to pay obligations. Regarding trust fund investments, see, for example, 42 U.S.C. §401 (Social Security Trust Funds), 5 U.S.C. §8348 (Civil Service Retirement and Disability Trust Fund), and 5 U.S.C. §8909 (Postal Service Retiree Health Benefit Fund).

[10] For example, see out-of-print CRS Report 95-1109, Authority to Tap Trust Funds and Establish Payment Priorities if the Debt Limit is not Increased, by Thomas J. Nicola and Morton Rosenberg (available from CRS upon request).

[11] Under-investing or disinvesting certain government funds provides room under the debt limit by freezing or reducing the amount of government debt held in these accounts in order to provide head room for more debt to be issued to the public to facilitate sufficient cash flow to pay obligations or to use receipts that would otherwise be invested in Treasury securities for purposes of paying other obligations.

[12] Congress formally authorized the additional powers to the Treasury Secretary under a "debt issuance suspension period" in the Omnibus Budget Reconciliation Act of 1986 (P.L. 99-509) and Thrift Savings Fund Investment Act of 1987 (P.L. 100-43).

[13] For a more detailed analysis of past Treasury actions surrounding the debt limit impasses of 1985, 1995-1996, and 2011, see the Appendix.

[14] Treasury also redeemed some of the Social Security Trust Funds' holdings of long-term securities to reimburse the General Fund for cash payments of benefits in September through November 1985. During this period, Treasury was unable to follow its normal procedure of issuing short-term securities to the trust funds and then redeeming short-term securities to reimburse the General Fund when it paid Social Security benefits.

[15] Treasury's Exchange Stabilization Fund buys and sells foreign currency to promote exchange rate stability and counter disorderly conditions in the foreign exchange market.

[16] As described in the Appendix, under normal procedures Treasury pays Social Security benefits from the General Fund and offsets this by redeeming an equivalent amount of the trust funds' holdings of government debt. In order to pay Social Security benefits, and depending on the government's cash position at the time, Treasury may need to issue new public debt to raise the cash needed to pay benefits. Treasury may be unable to issue new public debt, however, because of the debt limit. Social Security benefit payments may be delayed or jeopardized if the Treasury does not have enough cash on hand to pay benefits.

[17] The SFP has not been used since August 2011. Balances in the SFP account prior to that date can be found in Federal Reserve Bank, "Factors Affecting Reserve Balances," Table H.4.1, available at http://www.federalreserve.gov/releases/ h41/.

[18] Letter from Timothy F. Geithner, Secretary of the Treasury, to the Hon. Harry Reid, Senate Majority Leader, January 6, 2011, available at http://www.treasury.gov/connect/blog/ Pages/letter.aspx (hereinafter Treasury January 6th letter).

[19] Letter from Timothy F. Geithner, Secretary of the Treasury, to the Hon. John A. Boehner, Speaker of the House, May 2, 2011, available at http://www.treasury.gov/connect/blog/Documents/FINAL%20Debt%20Limit%20Letter%2005-02-2011%20Boehner.pdf (hereinafter Treasury May 2nd letter).

[20] For more information, see CRS Report R41811, State and Local Government Series (SLGS) Treasury Debt: A Description, by Steven Maguire and Jeffrey M. Stupak.

[21] Letter from Timothy F. Geithner, Secretary of the Treasury, to the Hon. Harry Reid, Senate Majority Leader, May 16, 2011, available at http://www.treasury.gov/connect/blog/Documents/20110516Letter%20to%20Congress.pdf (hereinafter Treasury May 16th letter).

[22] Letter from Richard L. Gregg, Fiscal Assistant Secretary, Department of the Treasury, to the Hon. John A. Boehner, Speaker of the House, August 24, 2011, available at http://www.treasury.gov/initiatives/Documents/ G%20Fund%20Letters.pdf and Letter to the Hon. Harry Reid, Senate majority leader, January 27, 2012, available at http://www.treasury.gov/initiatives/Documents/Debt%20Limit%20CSRDF%20Report%20to%20Reid.pdf.

[23] For more information on the provisions providing for the debt limit to be increased under the BCA, see CRS Report R41965, The Budget Control Act of 2011, by Bill Heniff Jr., Elizabeth Rybicki, and Shannon M. Mahan. Prior to the third debt limit increase, investments in the Government Securities Investment Fund (G-Fund) of the Federal Thrift Savings Plan were suspended from January 17 to January 27, 2012. The G-Fund was made whole on January 27, 2012. Letter from Timothy F. Geithner, Secretary of the Treasury, to the Hon. Harry Reid, Senate Majority Leader, January 17, 2012, available at http://www.treasury.gov/initiatives/Documents/011712TFGLettertoReid.pdf.

[24] Letter from Timothy F. Geithner, Secretary of the Treasury, to the Hon. Harry Reid, Senate Majority Leader, December 26, 2012, available at http://www.treasury.gov/connect/blog/Documents/ Sec%20Geithner%20LETTER%2012-26-2012%20Debt%20Limit.pdf.

[25] Letter from Timothy F. Geithner, Secretary of the Treasury, to the Hon. Harry Reid, Senate Majority Leader, December 31, 2012, available at http://www.treasury.gov/initiatives/Documents/ Sec%20Geithner%20Letter%20to%20Congress%2012-31-2012.pdf.

[26] Letter from Timothy F. Geithner, Secretary of the Treasury, to the Hon. John A. Boehner, Speaker of the House, January 15, 2013, available at http://www.treasury.gov/initiatives/Documents/1-15- 2013%20G%20Fund%20Debt%20Limit%20Letter.pdf.

[27] P.L. 113-3 provided for the debt limit to be increased on May 19, 2103 "to the extent that—(1) the face amount of obligations issued under chapter 31 of such title and the face amount of obligations whose principal and interest are guaranteed by the United States Government (except guaranteed obligations held by the Secretary of the Treasury) outstanding on May 19, 2013, exceeds (2) the face amount of such obligations outstanding on the date of the enactment of this Act. An obligation shall not be taken into account under paragraph (1) unless the issuance of such obligation was necessary to fund a commitment incurred by the Federal Government that required payment before May 19, 2013."

[28] Letter from Jacob J. Lew, Secretary of the Treasury, to the Hon. John A. Boehner, Speaker of the House, May 20, 2013, available at http://www.treasury.gov/initiatives/Documents/Debt%20Limit%20Letter%202%20Boehner%20May%2020%202013.pdf.

[29] Letter from Jacob J. Lew, Secretary of the Treasury, to the Hon. John A. Boehner, Speaker of the House, May 31, 2013, available at http://www.treasury.gov/initiatives/Documents/Debt%20Limit%20G%20Fund%2020130531%20Boehner.pdf.

[30] Letter from Jacob J. Lew, Secretary of the Treasury, to the Hon. John A. Boehner, Speaker of the House, October 1, 2013, available at http://www.treasury.gov/initiatives/Documents/ Treasury%20Letter%20to%20Congress_100113.pdf.

[31] Letter from Jacob J. Lew, Secretary of the Treasury, to the Hon. John A. Boehner, Speaker of the House, February 7, 2014, available at http://www.treasury.gov/initiatives/ Documents/Debt%20Limit%20Letter%20020714.pdf.

[32] Letter from Jacob J. Lew, Secretary of the Treasury, to the Hon. John A. Boehner, Speaker of the House, February 10, 2014, available at http://www.treasury.gov/initiatives/Documents/ 02102014%20CSRDF%20G%20Fund%20Letter.pdf.

[33] Letter from Jacob J. Lew, Secretary of the Treasury, to the Hon. John A. Boehner, Speaker of the House, March 13, 2015, available at http://www.treasury.gov/initiatives/ Documents/ Debt%20Limit%20Letter%2020150313.pdf.

[34] Ibid and Letter from Jacob J. Lew, Secretary of the Treasury, to the Hon. John A. Boehner, Speaker of the House, March 16, 2015, available at http://www.treasury.gov/initiatives /Documents/ Treasury%20Letter%20to%20Congress%20031615.pdf.

[35] Congressional Budget Office, Federal Debt and the Statutory Limit, March 2015, p. 1, available at http://www.cbo.gov/sites/default/files/cbofiles/attachments/49961-DebtLimit. pdf.

[36] For a discussion of how Treasury's cash management practices and borrowing costs were affected during previous debt limit event periods, see GAO, Delays Create Debt Management Challenges and Increase Uncertainty in the Treasury Market, GAO-11-203, February 2011, pp. 10-18.

[37] A more in-depth discussion of these proposals and their implications can be found in the section titled "Views on the Debt Limit, Prioritization, and Default."

[38] U.S. Congress, Senate Committee on Finance, Increase of Permanent Public Debt Limit, S.Rpt. 99-144, September 26, 1985. For more information, see out-of-print CRS Report 95-1109, Authority to Tap Trust Funds and Establish Payment Priorities if the Debt Limit is Not Increased, by Thomas J. Nicola and Morton Rosenberg (available from CRS upon request).

[39] Letter from GAO to the Hon. Bob Packwood, chairman of Senate Finance Committee, GAO B-138524, October 9, 1985, at http://redbook.gao.gov/14/fl0065142.php.

[40] While CRS has not located a list of established priorities to pay bills during a lapse in increasing the debt limit, OMB previously prepared a list of excepted functions that the government should continue to conduct during a government shutdown caused by a lapse in enacting appropriations. These priorities are based on a distinction between functions deemed essential and thus excepted, such as providing health care or air traffic control, and those deemed non-excepted. If it should become necessary to establish priorities to pay bills when the debt limit has not been increased, it is possible that the Secretary of the Treasury may look to this list of essential functions for some guidance. For OMB's guidance on what activities are essential during a shutdown, see Sylvia Burwell, "Memorandum for the Heads of Executive Departments and Agencies," Office of Management and Budget, September 17, 2013, http://www.whitehouse.gov/sites/default/files/omb/memoranda/2013/m-13-22.pdf. See also the later discussion in the section titled "Distinction Between a Debt Limit Crisis and a Government Shutdown."

[41] "Treasury: Proposals to 'Prioritize' Payments on U.S. Debt Not Workable: Would Not Prevent Default," Neal Wolin, Deputy Secretary of the Treasury, January 21, 2011, at http://www.treasury.gov/connect/blog/Pages/Proposals-toPrioritize-Payments-on-US-Debt-Not-Workable-Would-Not-Prevent-Default.aspx.

[42] Letter from Eric M. Thorson, Chair, Council of the Inspectors General on Financial Oversight, to Hon. Orrin G. Hatch, ranking Member, Committee on Finance, August 24, 2012, Enclosure 1, pp. 5-6, available at http://www.treasury.gov/about/organizational-structure/ig/Audit%20Reports%20and%20Testimonies/ Debt%20Limit%20Response%20(Final%20with%20Signature).pdf.

[43] U.S. Congress, Hearing of the Senate Committee on Finance, The Debt Limit, 113th Congress, 1st Session, October 10, 2013. Transcript available on CQ.com at http://www.cq.com/ doc/congressionaltranscripts-4359941.

[44] Letter from Alastair M. Fitzpayne, Assistant Secretary for Legislative Affairs, to Hon. Jeb Hensarling, Chairman, Committee on Financial Services, May 7, 2014, available at http://www.cq.com/pdf/4473840.

[45] Title X of the Congressional Budget and Impoundment Control Act of 1974 (P.L. 93-344; 88 Stat. 297, at 332, and subsequently amended; 2 U.S.C. Chapter 17B, §681 et seq.). The act grew out of extended conflict over spending priorities between Congress and the Richard M. Nixon Administration, including over "policy" impoundments, where the Administration sought to not spend funds associated with disfavored programs. The act generally has been interpreted as being intended to protect congressional budget decisions and priorities, as manifest in statutes, from deviations by the President, OMB, and agency officials. For discussion, see Allen Schick, Congress and Money: Budgeting, Spending, and Taxing (Washington, DC: Urban Institute, 1980), pp. 17-49, 401-412.

[46] The ICA does not prohibit impoundments, but rather controls them. Among other things, the ICA established a mechanism for the President, the Director of OMB, the head of an agency, or any officer or employee to propose deferrals, for which the President is required to transmit a special message to each chamber of Congress with certain information. In addition, a deferral may not be proposed for any period of time extending beyond the end of the fiscal year in which the special message is transmitted.

[47] For related discussion, see Laurence H. Tribe, "Guest Post on the Debt Ceiling by Laurence Tribe," July 16, 2011, at http://www.dorfonlaw.org/2011/07/guest-post-on-debt-ceiling-by-laurence.html; and Neil H. Buchanan and Michael C. Dorf, "How to Choose the Least Unconstitutional Option: Lessons for the President (and Others) From the Debt Ceiling Standoff," Columbia Law Review, vol. 112, no. 6, October 2012, pp. 1175-1243, at http://www.columbialawreview.org/wp-content/uploads/2012/10/Buchanan-Dorf.pdf.

[48] See related discussion in ibid. As noted earlier, the ICA provides that deferrals may not be proposed for any period of time extending beyond the end of the fiscal year in which the special message is transmitted. However, a debt limit impasse may create a situation in which it is impossible for the President or an agency official to comply with all aspects of existing law at the same time. Neil H. Buchanan and Michael C. Dorf characterized a debt ceiling standoff as a "trilemma," in which officials in the executive branch are offered "three unconstitutional options: ignore the debt ceiling and unilaterally issue new bonds, thus usurping Congress's borrowing power; unilaterally raise taxes, thus usurping Congress's taxing power; or unilaterally cut spending, thus usurping Congress's spending power." Ibid., p. 1175.

[49] See Office of Management and Budget, "Background Material on Prior Debt Ceiling Crises," memorandum from Roz Rettman to Bob Damus, August 2, 1995, pp. 4-5, as paginated within the document, which is available as pp. 7-11 of a PDF file, at http://www.clintonlibrary.gov/_previous/KAGAN%20COUNSEL/Counsel%20-%20Box%20006%20-%20Folder%20011.pdf. The OMB memorandum's author and recipient were senior career officials at OMB at the time. Elena Kagan currently is serving

as Associate Justice of the U.S. Supreme Court. In 1995-1996, she served as Associate White House Counsel under President Clinton. Access to certain records from Justice Kagan's time in the Office of White House Counsel is provided at the Clinton Library website.

[50] 31 U.S.C. §1512, a provision of the Antideficiency Act, for example, states that appropriations for a definite period must be apportioned by such things as months, activities, or a combination of them to avoid obligation at a rate that would indicate a necessity of a deficiency or supplemental appropriations for the period. While apportionment commonly is used to control the rate at which agencies are allowed to obligate funds such as by placing orders and signing contracts, the text of Section 1512 also provides that it may be used to avoid expending funds.

[51] See 2 U.S.C. §§681-692. During the period leading up to enactment of the Impoundment Control Act of 1974, the Nixon Administration used apportionment authority as a tool ultimately to limit outlays to conform to the President's budgetary priorities. Several lawsuits were brought to challenge the President's authority not to expend funds that Congress had appropriated, and some lower courts held that the President lacked this authority. The Supreme Court did not address the merits of this issue.

[52] Generally, funds that have been proposed for deferral or rescission may be withheld from obligation for 45 days of continuous legislative session (excluding periods of more than three days when Congress is not in session), after which period the funds must be released unless Congress enacts a joint resolution to acquiesce in whole or in part to these requests. Congress sometimes responds to presidential deferral or rescission requests by acting on bills to defer or rescind different budget authorities from the ones that the President has proposed. Because deferrals or rescissions proposed by the President do not take effect unless Congress acquiesces to them, Congress as a matter of law has the final say on these matters. In practice, however, funds that are subject to these presidential requests often are withheld for long periods because of congressional recesses, which as noted above are not counted for purposes of the ICA. For more information, see CRS Report RL33869, Rescission Actions Since 1974: Review and Assessment of the Record, by Virginia A. McMurtry, p. 2.

[53] Discretionary spending is provided in, and controlled by, annual appropriations acts, which fund many of the routine activities commonly associated with such federal government functions as running executive branch agencies, congressional offices and agencies, and international operations of the government. Mandatory spending includes federal government spending on entitlement programs as well as other budget outlays controlled by laws other than appropriations acts. Mandatory spending also includes appropriated entitlements, such as Medicaid and certain veterans' programs, which are funded in annual appropriations acts. For more information, see CRS Report RS20129, Entitlements and Appropriated Entitlements in the Federal Budget Process, by Bill Heniff Jr.

[54] For example, because federal, state, and local government finances are linked by various intergovernmental transfers, late payment or nonpayment of federal obligations to states could affect the budgets and finances of local governments, such as school districts, counties, and municipalities.

[55] 31 U.S.C. §3902. The Prompt Payment Act generally requires federal agencies to pay interest on any payments they fail to make by the date(s) specified in a contract or within 30 days of a receipt of a proper invoice. For more information, see the section titled "The Prompt Payment Act" in CRS Report R41230, Legal Protections for Subcontractors on Federal Prime Contracts, by Kate M. Manuel.

[56] 26 U.S.C. §6611.

[57] For information about the balances of all federal trust funds, see CRS Report R41328, Federal Trust Funds and the Budget, by Mindy R. Levit.

[58] CBO, The Economic and Budget Outlook: An Update, August 1995, p. 49.

[59] In the event of a funding hiatus, the Antideficiency Act nevertheless allows an exception for agencies to incur obligations for emergencies involving the safety of human life or the protection of property. For a discussion, see CRS Report RL34680, Shutdown of the Federal Government: Causes, Processes, and Effects, coordinated by Clinton T. Brass.

[60] While this passage indicates that a delay in increasing the debt limit has the potential to postpone the payment of Social Security benefits, among other benefits, Social Security benefits have been paid on time during past debt limit crises. Non-marketable securities can be redeemed on demand. GAO, A New Approach to the Public Debt Legislation Should be Considered, FGMSD-79-58, September 1979, pp. 17-18, http://archive.gao.gov/f0302/110373.pdf.

[61] Ibid.

[62] GDP = consumption + investment + government spending + (exports − imports). If government spending declines, then GDP will also decline by definition, all else equal.

[63] The Treasury Borrowing Advisory Committee is a group of senior representatives from investment funds and banks that presents its observations on the overall strength of the U.S. economy and provides recommendations on a variety of technical debt management issues to the Treasury Department.

[64] More information on the Treasury Borrowing Advisory Committee can be found at http://www.treasury.gov/resource-center/data-chart-center/quarterly-refunding/Pages/default.aspx.

[65] Letter from Matthew E. Zames, Chairman of Treasury Borrowing Advisory Committee, to Timothy F. Geithner, April 25, 2011, available at http://www.sifma.org/issues/item.aspx?id=25013.

[66] This section was written by Marc Labonte, Specialist in Macroeconomic Policy.

[67] The absence of large declines in financial markets could be interpreted as a market belief that a default would not have serious effects or that "brinkmanship" is unlikely to result in a default because the debt limit will ultimately be raised.

[68] The fact that growth accelerated in the following quarter suggests that the debt limit impasse did not have prolonged effects on the economy.

[69] U.S. Treasury, The Potential Macroeconomic Effect of Debt Ceiling Brinkmanship, Oct. 2013.

[70] Standard & Poors, "United States of America Long-Term Rating Lowered to AA+ Due to Political Risks, Rising Debt Burden; Outlook Negative," August 5, 2011, available at http://www.standardandpoors.com/ratings/articles/en/us/ ?assetID=1245316529563.

[71] There was also a marked decline in Treasury yields in August 2011; since this was not matched by a decline in private yields, it caused the spread between Treasury yields and private yields to widen. Based on the timing, this movement appears to have been in response to the downgrade rather than the debt limit impasse, and so is attributable to the debt limit impasse only in the sense that it triggered the downgrade.

[72] This estimate includes only costs incurred in FY2011. It does not include any additional interest costs incurred in future years on outstanding securities related to this borrowing. See Government Accountability Office, Analysis of 2011-2012 Actions Taken and Effect of Delayed Increase on Borrowing Costs, report number GAO-12-701, July 23, 2012.

[73] The circumstances under which CDS on Treasury securities would be triggered are described in International Swaps and Derivatives Association, CDS on US Sovereign Debt- FAQ, updated Oct. 9, 2013.

[74] Abigail Moses, "U.S. Credit-Default Swaps Trading Surges 80% as Debt Deadline Approaches," Bloomberg, July 28, 2011. For more information on Treasury CDS in 2011 and the pricing of CDS, see CRS Report R41932, Treasury Securities and the U.S. Sovereign Credit Default Swap Market, by D. Andrew Austin and Rena S. Miller.

75 Markit, Biggest Credit Movers, Oct. 10, 2013, http://www.markit.com/assets/en/docs/commentary/markit-movers/Biggest%20Credit%20Movers%20Import/BigMovers_ 1010 13.pdf.

[76] Letter from Timothy F. Geithner, Secretary of the Treasury, to the Hon. John A. Boehner, Speaker of the U.S. House of Representatives, January 14, 2013, available at http://www.treasury.gov/connect/blog/Documents/1-14-13%20Debt%20 Limit%20FINAL %20LETTER%20Boehner.pdf.

[77] "President Obama Holds the Final Press Conference of His First Term," January 14, 2013, available at http://www.whitehouse.gov/blog/2013/01/14/president-obama-holds-final-press-conference-his-first-term.

[78] Peter G. Peterson Foundation's 2012 Fiscal Summit, Speaker Boehner's Address on the Economy, Debt Limit, and American Jobs, May 15, 2012, available at http://www.speaker.gov/speech/full-text-speaker-boehners-addresseconomy-debt-limit-and-american-jobs.

[79] Cooper, Helene, "Obama and House Republicans Offer Taste of Renewed Fight Over the Debt Ceiling," New York Times, May 16, 2012.

[80] Davidson, Paul, "Economy still in a deep hole, Bernanke says," USA Today, February 4, 2011.

[81] U.S. Congress, Senate Committee on the Budget, Challenges for the U.S. Economic Recovery, Testimony of Mark Zandi, February 3, 2011, available at http://budget.senate.gov/democratic/testimony/2011/ Zandi_Senate_Budget_2_3_2011.pdf.

[82] Marron, Donald, "Debt Ceiling: Geithner Won't Let Us Default," CNNMoney.com, January 19, 2011.

[83] The potential effects of reaching the debt limit on financial markets are further discussed in the section titled "Potential Economic and Financial Effects."

[84] This section contains descriptions of legislation that has been either reported by committee or considered in either the House or the Senate as it relates to the debt limit since the enactment of P.L. 113-3 (H.R. 325). Other bills related to prioritization of payments in the event the debt limit is reached have been introduced in the House and the Senate.

[85] CRS calculations based on CBO, Updated Budget Projections: 2015 to 2025, March 2015, Table 4.

[86] Office of Management and Budget, Budget of the U.S. Government, Fiscal Year 2016, The Budget, Table S-13, available at https://www.whitehouse.gov/sites/default/files/omb/budget/fy2016/assets/tables.pdf.

[87] Ibid., Table S-1.

[88] The Senate agreed to a budget resolution on March 27, 2015 (S.Con.Res. 11). However, accompanying documents do not provide information on the level of debt subject to limit. The text of the resolution specifies a public debt level of $19,009 billion at the end of FY2016 and $21,207 billion at the end of FY2025. A small amount of public debt is not subject to the debt limit.

[89] CBO, Federal Debt and Interest Costs, December 2010, p. 23, available at http://www.cbo.gov/ftpdocs/119xx/ doc11999/12-14-FederalDebt.pdf.

[90] For more information, see CRS Report RS21519, Legislative Procedures for Adjusting the Public Debt Limit: A Brief Overview, by Bill Heniff Jr.

[91] Under the most recent projections, the federal budget is expected to remain in deficit through FY2025 under current law. CBO, Updated Budget Projections: 2015 to 2025, March 2015, Table 4.

[92] Treasury redeemed some of the Social Security Trust Funds' holdings of long-term securities to reimburse the General Fund for cash payments of benefits in September through November 1985. During this period, the Treasury was unable to follow its normal procedure of issuing short-term securities to the trust funds and then redeeming short-term securities to reimburse the General Fund when it paid Social Security benefits.

[93] Letter from Charles A. Bowsher, Comptroller General of the United States, to the Hon. James R. Jones, chairman, Subcommittee on Social Security, House Committee on Ways and Means, December 5, 1985, GAO B-221077.2, http://archive.gao.gov/d12t3/128621.pdf.

[94] Ibid.

[95] GAO, Debt Ceiling Options, AIMD-96-20R, December 7, 1995, http://archive.gao.gov/paprpdfl/155750.pdf.

[96] Treasury's Exchange Stabilization Fund buys and sells foreign currency to promote exchange rate stability and counter disorderly conditions in the foreign exchange market.

[97] As described later in this Appendix, under normal procedures Treasury pays Social Security benefits from the General Fund and offsets this by redeeming an equivalent amount of the trust funds' holdings of government debt. In order to pay Social Security benefits, and depending on the government's cash position at the time, Treasury may need to issue new public debt to raise the cash needed to pay benefits. Treasury may be unable to issue new public debt, however, because of the debt limit. Social Security benefit payments may be delayed or jeopardized if the Treasury does not have enough cash on hand to pay benefits.

[98] See 42 U.S.C. §1320b-15.

[99] U.S. Social Security Administration, "Program Legislation Enacted in Early 1996," Social Security Bulletin, vol. 59, no. 2, Summer 1996, p. 65, at http://www.ssa.gov/policy/docs/ssb/v59n2/index.html.

[100] Treasury January 6th letter.

[101] Letter from Timothy F. Geithner, Secretary of the Treasury, to the Hon. Harry Reid, Senate Majority Leader, April 4, 2011, available at http://www.treasury.gov/connect/blog/Documents/FINAL%20Letter%2004-04- 2011%20Reid%20Debt%20Limit.pdf.

[102] Treasury May 2nd letter.

[103] For more information, see CRS Report R41811, State and Local Government Series (SLGS) Treasury Debt: A Description, by Steven Maguire and Jeffrey M. Stupak.

[104] Treasury May 16th letter.

[105] Letter from Richard L. Gregg, Fiscal Assistant Secretary, Department of the Treasury, to the Hon. John A. Boehner, Speaker of the House, August 24, 2011, available at http://www.treasury.gov/initiatives/Documents/ G%20Fund%20Letters.pdf and Letter to the Hon. Harry Reid, Senate Majority Leader, January 27, 2012, available at http://www.treasury.gov/initiatives/Documents/Debt%20Limit%20CSRDF%20Report%20to%20Reid.pdf.

[106] For more information on the provisions providing for the debt limit to be increased under the BCA, see CRS Report R41965, The Budget Control Act of 2011, by Bill Heniff Jr., Elizabeth Rybicki, and Shannon M. Mahan. Prior to the third debt limit increase, investments in the Government Securities Investment Fund (G-Fund) of the Federal Thrift Savings Plan were suspended from January 17 to January 27, 2012. The G-Fund was made

whole on January 27, 2012. Letter from Timothy F. Geithner, Secretary of the Treasury, to the Hon. Harry Reid, Senate Majority Leader, January 17, 2012, available at http://www.treasury.gov/initiatives/Documents/011712TFGLettertoReid.pdf.

[107] Letter from Timothy F. Geithner, Secretary of the Treasury, to the Hon. Harry Reid, Senate Majority Leader, December 26, 2012, available at http://www.treasury.gov/connect/blog/Documents/Sec%20Geithner%20LETTER%2012-26-2012%20Debt%20Limit.pdf.

[108] Letter from Timothy F. Geithner, Secretary of the Treasury, to the Hon. Harry Reid, Senate Majority Leader, January 6, 2011, p. 4.

[109] Ibid., pp. 1, 3.

[110] ABC News This Week, Transcript: White House Adviser Austan Goolsbee, January 2, 2011, at http://abcnews.go.com/ThisWeek/week-transcript-white-house-adviser-austan-goolsbee/story?id=12522822.

[111] Treasury Secretary Geithner letter, January 6, 2011, p. 4.

[112] Neal Wolin, Deputy Secretary of the Treasury, "Treasury: Proposals to 'Prioritize' Payments on U.S. Debt Not Workable; Would Not Prevent Default," January 21, 2011, at http://www.treasury.gov/connect/blog/Pages/Proposalsto-Prioritize-Payments-on-US-Debt-Not-Workable-Would-Not-Prevent-Default.aspx.

[113] Treasury Secretary Geithner letter, January 6, 2011, p. 4.

[114] Senator Jim DeMint, "More Spending is a Threat to America," Politico, January 24, 2011, available at http://www.politico.com/news/stories/0111/48020.html.

[115] Senator Pat Toomey, "Senator Toomey Sends Letter to Secretary Geithner on the Debt Limit," press release, February 2, 2011, http://toomey.senate.gov/record.cfm?id=330828&.

[116] Representative Dean Heller was sworn in to the U.S. Senate on May 9, 2011, to fill the seat of former Senator John Ensign who had resigned.

[117] These are examples of legislation introduced as of February 15, 2011. Some of this legislation has been considered as amendments to other legislation and were tabled or withdrawn. Other legislation has been subsequently introduced, however, this is not intended to be a legislative tracking report. Therefore not all bills are included in the list above.

[118] Social Security income comes from several sources: (1) payroll taxes paid by workers and employers; (2) federal income taxes paid by some beneficiaries on a portion of their benefits; (3) reimbursements from the General Fund to the trust funds for a variety of purposes; and (4) interest income from trust fund investments. Interest income is paid as a credit from the General Fund to the trust funds, in the form of additional nonmarketable government securities.

[119] Generally, the trust funds' long-term securities have maturities ranging from 1 to 15 years and normally mature in June of the applicable year.

[120] For a detailed discussion, see Social Security Administration, Office of the Chief Actuary, Social Security Trust Fund Investment Policies and Practices, Actuarial Note Number 142, January 1999, http://www.ssa.gov/OACT/ NOTES/pdf_notes/note142.pdf (hereinafter cited as SSA Actuarial Note Number 142).

[121] Social Security relies on accumulated trust fund assets to help pay benefits and administrative expenses when the program runs a cash deficit. Social Security benefits scheduled under current law can be paid in full and on time as long as there is a sufficient balance in the trust funds. The combined Social Security trust funds are projected to have a positive balance until 2033, when trust fund assets are projected to be exhausted under the intermediate assumptions of the Social Security Board of Trustees. For SSA's projections of Social Security Trust Fund operations, see 2014 Annual Report of the Board of Trustees of the

Federal Old-Age and Survivors Insurance and Federal Disability Insurance Trust Funds, Washington, DC, July 28, 2014, http://www.socialsecurity.gov/OACT/TR/2014/tr2014.pdf. In addition, see CRS Report RL33028, Social Security: The Trust Fund, by Dawn Nuschler and Gary Sidor and CRS Report R43318, Social Security Disability Insurance (DI) Trust Fund: Background and Solvency Issues, by William R. Morton.

[122] P.L. 111-312, as amended by P.L. 112-78 and P.L. 112-96, made no change to the Social Security payroll tax rate for employers (6.2%) or to the amount of wages and net self-employment income subject to the Social Security payroll tax.

[123] See P.L. 111-312, Title VI (Temporary Employee Payroll Tax Cut), at http://www.gpo.gov/fdsys/pkg/PLAW111publ312/pdf/PLAW-111publ312.pdf.

[124] SSA Actuarial Note Number 142, p. 3.

In: Debt Limit Impasses
Editor: Phil Frazier

ISBN: 978-1-63484-335-5
© 2016 Nova Science Publishers, Inc.

Chapter 2

DEBT LIMIT: MARKET RESPONSE TO RECENT IMPASSES UNDERSCORES NEED TO CONSIDER ALTERNATIVE APPROACHES[*]

United States Government Accountability Office

WHY GAO DID THIS STUDY

GAO prepared this report as part of its continuing efforts to assist Congress in identifying and addressing debt management challenges related to delays in raising the debt limit. This report examines the effect of delays in raising the debt limit in 2013 on (1) the broader financial system and (2) Treasury debt and cash management and (3) examines alternative approaches to delegating borrowing authority that could minimize future disruptions. To address these objectives, GAO interviewed Treasury officials and market participants across different sectors and analyzed financial market data. GAO also hosted a private online forum where experts provided input on different proposals.

---

[*] This is an edited, reformatted and augmented version of the United States Government Accountability Office publication, GAO-15-476, dated July 2015.

WHAT GAO RECOMMENDS

To avoid disruptions to the Treasury market and to help inform fiscal policy debate in a timely way, Congress should consider alternative approaches that better link decisions about the debt limit with decisions about spending and revenue at the time those decisions are made, such as those described in this report. However, if Congress chooses to continue to temporarily suspend the debt limit, it should consider providing Treasury with more flexibility than provided under the current approach, which effectively requires Treasury to return its cash balance to roughly the same level it was immediately prior to the suspension.

Treasury agreed with GAO's findings regarding the effects of the debt limit on financial markets and indicated that it saw advantages in the alternative approaches described in this report.

Through interviews of budget and policy experts and an interactive web forum, GAO identified three potential approaches to delegating borrowing authority. Each option met the criteria of (1) minimizing disruptions to the market and (2) linking decisions about debt to decisions about spending and revenue at the time that those decisions are made. All of the options also maintain congressional control and oversight over federal borrowing.

Option 1: Link Action on the Debt Limit to the Budget Resolution

This is a variation of a previously used approach under which legislation raising the debt limit to the level envisioned in the Congressional Budget Resolution would be spun off and either be deemed to have passed or be voted on immediately thereafter.

Option 2: Provide the Administration with the Authority to Increase the Debt Limit, Subject to a Congressional Motion of Disapproval

This is a variation of an approach contained in the Budget Control Act of 2011. Congress would give the administration the authority to propose a change in the debt limit, which would take effect absent enactment of a joint resolution of disapproval within a specified time frame.

Option 3: Delegating Broad Authority to the Administration to Borrow as Necessary to Fund Enacted Laws

This is an approach used in some other countries: delegate to the administration the authority to borrow such sums as necessary to fund implementation of the laws duly enacted by Congress and the President. Since laws that affect federal spending and revenue that create the need for debt already require adoption by the Congress, Congress would still maintain control over the amount of federal borrowing.

WHAT GAO FOUND

During the 2013 debt limit impasse, investors reported taking the unprecedented action of systematically avoiding certain Treasury securities—those that matured around the dates when the Department of the Treasury (Treasury) projected it would exhaust the extraordinary measures that it uses to manage federal debt when it is at the limit. For the affected Treasury securities, these actions resulted in both a dramatic increase in rates and a decline in liquidity in the secondary market where securities are traded among investors. In addition, there were also unusually low levels of demand at the relevant auctions and additional borrowing costs to Treasury. Treasury securities are one of the lowest cost and widely used forms of collateral for financial transactions, and because of this, disruptions to the Treasury market from the 2013 debt limit impasse extended into other markets, such as short-term financing.

Investors told GAO that they are now prepared to take similar steps to systematically avoid certain Treasury securities during future debt limit impasses. Market participants with whom GAO spoke said market reaction to future impasses could be more severe, in part because of changes in market practices since the financial crisis and in part because of contingency plans that many investors now have in place. Separately, there was an effort across the financial sector to develop a contingency plan to address the potential of a delayed Treasury payment, although industry groups emphasized that even a temporary delay in payment could undermine confidence in the full faith and credit of the United States and therefore cause significant damage to markets for Treasury securities and other assets. This would affect not only institutions, but also individuals.

While increased rates on Treasury securities in the secondary market affect the amount of return on investment for private investors, changes in the rates paid at Treasury auctions affect the amount that Treasury—and ultimately the American taxpayer—pays in interest on federal debt. GAO's analysis indicates that the additional borrowing costs that Treasury incurred rose rapidly in the final weeks and days leading up to the October 2013 deadline when Treasury projected it would exhaust its extraordinary measures. GAO estimated the total increased borrowing costs incurred through September 30, 2014, on securities issued by Treasury during the 2013 debt limit impasse. These estimates ranged from roughly $38 million to more than $70 million, depending on the specifications used.

Recently, Congress has temporarily suspended the debt limit. At the end of past debt limit suspensions, Treasury sharply reduced its cash balance to match the cash that it had on hand just prior to each suspension to ensure that it complied with legal limitations. Treasury reduced its cash balance in part by reducing the amount of Treasury bills outstanding, which can be disruptive to markets that transact in Treasury bills. Further, maintaining low levels of cash, even temporarily, conflicts with Treasury's new policy to hold more cash to mitigate the risk that Treasury will be unable to access funding markets due to unforeseen events—such as natural disasters—as recommended by the Treasury Borrowing Advisory Committee. Managing cash balances at a prudent level is consistent with standards for internal control on responding to risk.

Option 1: Link Action on the Debt Limit to the Budget Resolution

Possible design outcomes include

- making clear the relationship between spending and revenue decisions in the budget resolution and the debt implied by those decisions;
- giving Congress the ability to take more immediate action to affect debt by incorporating changes to revenue and spending at the time that Congress passes its annual budget plan; and

- minimizing potential disruptions to the market by shifting the timing of the debate so that it occurs before debt is already at the limit;

Design issues to consider include (1) how should the debt limit be linked to the budget resolution and how would voting occur, and (2) how should this policy account for legislative and economic changes not included in the budget resolution.

Option 2: Provide the Administration with the Authority to Increase the Debt Limit, Subject to a Congressional Motion of Disapproval

Possible design outcomes include

- preserving Congress's ability to directly debate the current trajectory of federal debt;
- reducing the likelihood of market disruption and damage to the economy by changing the results of a lack of congressional action from a potential default to a debt limit increase;
- being viewed by some as insufficiently linking congressional decisions about spending and revenue to the impact on debt.

Design issues to be considered include (1) should Congress specify criteria or require accompanying explanatory information for proposed debt limit increases and, if so, what should they be; and (2) how should Congress structure the vote on a joint resolution of disapproval, including how much time Congress should be afforded to debate and pass a motion of disapproval before a change to the debt limit takes effect.

Option 3: Delegating Broad Authority to the Administration to Borrow as Necessary to Fund Enacted Laws

Possible design outcomes include
- removing the dangers that accompany the fear of default by the U.S. government by ensuring Treasury has the authority it needs to borrow to fund all previously authorized spending;

- permitting flexibility with respect to changes in the economy and legislation; and
- being viewed by some as having not enough focus on the link between spending and revenue decisions and the level of debt incurred.

Design issues to be considered include (1) what form should congressional oversight of Treasury debt management take in light of this delegation of authority; and (2) what reports might be required from Treasury, and at what frequency.

ABBREVIATIONS

ARMA	autoregressive-moving average
BCA	Budget Control Act of 2011
CBO	Congressional Budget Office
CSRDF	Civil Service Retirement and Disability Fund
DISP	debt issuance suspension period
ESF	Exchange Stabilization Fund
Fed Funds	Federal Funds
FFB	Federal Financing Bank
GARCH	generalized autoregressive conditional heteroskedasticity
GDP	gross domestic product
GCF	General Collateral Finance
G Fund	Government Securities Investment Fund
GSE	government sponsored enterprise
LIBOR	London Interbank Offered Rate
OLS	ordinary least squares
OMB	Office of Management and Budget
Postal Benefits Fund	Postal Service Retiree Health Benefits Fund
Recovery Act	American Recovery and Reinvestment Act of 2009
Repo	Repurchase Agreement
SIFMA	Securities Industry and Financial Markets Association
SLGS	State and Local Government Series
TIPS	Treasury Inflation-Protected Securities

| TMPG | Treasury Market Practices Group |
| Treasury | Department of the Treasury |

* * *

July 9, 2015

Report to the Congress

U.S. Treasury securities play a vital role in the U.S. and global financial markets, owing in part to their large, liquid, and transparent market and to the confidence investors have that debt backed by the full faith and credit of the United States will be honored. This can be seen by the exceptionally strong demand for U.S. Treasury securities during times of economic uncertainty around the world. Because Treasury securities are viewed as one of the safest assets in the world, they are broadly held by individuals—including in pension funds or mutual funds—and by institutions and central banks for use in everyday transactions. They serve as the equivalent of cash for financial institutions and corporate treasurers, are one of the cheapest and one of the most widely used forms of collateral for financial transactions, and are the basis for pricing many other financial products, such as corporate bonds, derivatives, and mortgages.

High demand for Treasury securities helps the Department of the Treasury (Treasury) meet its goal of financing the government at the lowest cost over time. Because the market for Treasury securities is large and liquid, trading can generally be completed at will, and there is only a slight difference in the price at which investors are willing to buy and sell the security in the secondary market. Both at auction and in the secondary market, investors are willing to pay more for the liquidity that Treasury securities offer, which contributes to lower borrowing costs for Treasury. Conversely, anything that decreases demand for Treasury securities or makes them less liquid could increase the cost of borrowing for Treasury. We have previously reported that delays in raising the debt limit—a legal limit on the amount of federal debt that can be outstanding at one time—has created uncertainty and disruptions in the Treasury market and challenges for Treasury debt and cash management.[1]

While the debt limit restricts Treasury's authority to borrow, it does not restrict Congress's ability to enact spending and revenue legislation that affects the level of debt or otherwise constrain fiscal policy. Congress usually votes on increasing the debt limit after fiscal policy decisions affecting federal borrowing have begun to take effect. In other words, Congress can commit to future federal spending that Treasury does not yet have sufficient borrowing authority to fund. We previously noted that this approach to raising the debt limit does not facilitate timely debate over specific tax or spending proposals and their effect on debt, and can limit the range of options Congress has to effect an immediate change on the trajectory of federal debt. We previously reported that Congress should consider ways to better link decisions about the debt limit with decisions about spending and revenue to avoid an impasse and potential disruptions to the Treasury market and to help inform the fiscal policy debate in a timely way.

On May 17, 2013, the Secretary of the Treasury notified Congress that Treasury would begin to take actions that depart from normal debt management operations to avoid breaching the limit. Treasury refers to these actions as "extraordinary measures." On September 25, 2013, the Secretary notified Congress that Treasury estimated that these extraordinary measures would be exhausted no later than October 17, 2013. On October 17, 2013, Congress passed and the President signed the Continuing Appropriations Act, 2014, which suspended the debt limit through February 7, 2014.[2] Rather than set a dollar limit, under a suspension Treasury is allowed to borrow as necessary to fund obligations during the suspension period.

We prepared this report under the Comptroller General's authority to conduct evaluations on his own initiative as part of continuing efforts to assist Congress in identifying and addressing debt management challenges related to delays in raising the debt limit. The objectives of this report are to examine the effect of delays in raising the debt limit in 2013 on (1) the broader financial system and (2) Treasury debt and cash management and (3) to examine alternative approaches to delegating borrowing authority that would tie decisions about the debt limit to the spending and revenue decisions that lead to debt and also could minimize future disruptions in the Treasury market.

To examine the effects of the debt limit on financial markets, we interviewed more than two dozen private sector market participants and observers to obtain their views and to learn about any contingency plans they developed. We also interviewed Treasury officials and Federal Reserve staff. We selected market participants to ensure a diversity of viewpoints, taking into consideration market sector, share of the Treasury market, and recommendations of market experts. Interviewees outside the Treasury and the Federal Reserve were representatives from six primary dealers, three commercial banks, seven money market mutual funds and bond funds, three clearing banks, the three largest rating agencies in the United States, a private asset manager, managers of one of the world's largest derivative exchanges, and a widely recognized expert and commentator on the Treasury market. The views expressed in these interviews are not generalizable to all market participants.

To assess the effect of the debt limit impasse that was resolved in October 2013—hereafter referred to as the October 2013 impasse—on secondary markets for Treasury securities and on markets for private securities, we analyzed data on rates on Treasury securities in the secondary market, repurchase agreements, and nonfinancial commercial paper, and data on the amount of financial commercial paper outstanding. We used publicly available data including Treasury's Monthly Statement of Public Debt and Daily Treasury Statement to calculate the amount of principal and interest on Treasury securities that was due from October 17, 2013, to November 15, 2013, when Treasury projected that it would exhaust its extraordinary measures.

To estimate the effect of the debt limit impasse in October 2013 on the borrowing costs of the U.S. government, we used econometric models to estimate yield premiums on Treasury securities associated with indicators of the perceived risk of disruptions in principal and interest payments due to the impasse. For these models, we used (1) daily data on searches of terms related to the debt limit impasse obtained from Google for the period from February 5, 2013, to October 16, 2013, and (2) daily counts of news articles that used terms related to the debt limit impasse obtained from Bloomberg News Trends data for the same period. Google Trends data measures the frequency of searches on Google for various phrases—in our case, searches related to the debt limit—which can serve as a proxy for market concern over the political impasse. The Google search index has been used successfully in other studies to capture changes in general public interest in an issue, but general public interest in the debt limit impasse may vary in systematic ways from the perceptions of market participants whose decisions affect prices.[3] Bloomberg News Trends data, on the other hand, counts debt-limit related news gathered from some of the same sources that populate news tickers on Bloomberg terminals and thus have a direct relationship with materials that are likely to contribute to market participants' risk assessments. Bloomberg News Trends data, however, are smaller in volume than Google search data and reflect the judgment of a comparatively small number of people (i.e., the journalists and editors that produce the stories) about how newsworthy the issue is. We applied estimates of increases to interest costs attributable to the debt limit to Treasury auctions held during the relevant period to estimate the direct costs to

Treasury. For this part of the analysis, we used daily data on Treasury auctions for the period from February 5, 2013 to October 16, 2013.

We selected eight economists external to GAO with relevant expertise to review our econometric approach and assess its strengths and limitations. Before selecting these experts, we reviewed potential sources of conflicts of interest, and we determined that the experts we selected did not have any material conflicts of interest for the purpose of reviewing our work. We received comments on our methodology from five of the selected experts. The other three were not available to participate in our study. Those that responded agreed with our general approach and provided technical comments for us to consider. To address these comments, we either modified our econometric approach or disclosed additional limitations of our approach.

The results of the models used in this report to estimate the additional borrowing costs to Treasury resulting from the 2013 debt limit impasse are not comparable to estimates for prior debt limit impasses that we published in past reports, which used different models.[4] The approach that we used in this report offered us a number of advantages. Most notably, it allowed us to model the escalation of the 2013 impasse on a day-by-day, auction-by-auction basis and to estimate when the additional borrowing costs to Treasury were incurred. With this modeling approach, we were able to capture the increases in Treasury yields in the days and weeks before Congress and the President resolved the impasse. See appendix II for more details on how we estimated increased borrowing costs and the limitations associated with this analysis.

To identify and examine alternative approaches to delegating borrowing authority, we interviewed budget and legislative experts, including former congressional staff, former Congressional Budget Office (CBO) directors and Office of Management and Budget (OMB) staff, and other congressional observers from a range of policy research organizations. We also reviewed all legislation pertaining to the debt limit introduced in the 112th and 113th Congresses, as well as congressional testimony on the debt limit since 2011. Based on the interviews and analysis as well as our previous work on the debt limit, we identified three policy options that could potentially minimize disruptions in the Treasury market and that link decisions about the debt limit to decisions about spending and revenue.

To obtain greater insight on these policy options, we hosted a private Web forum where selected experts participated in an interactive discussion on the various policy proposals and commented on the technical feasibility and merits of each option. We selected experts to invite to the forum based on their experience with budget and debt issues in various capacities (government officials, former congressional staff, and policy researchers), as well as on their knowledge of the debt limit, as demonstrated through published articles and congressional testimony since 2011. We also sought to include a range of political perspectives by taking into consideration factors such as an expert's past political appointments. The forum was open to participants from December 1 to 15, 2014, and we received comments from 17 of the experts invited to the forum. We determined that the 17 participants represented the full range of political perspectives. We analyzed the results of the forum to identify key factors that policymakers should consider when evaluating different policy options. Although these results are not generalizable to all experts with relevant expertise, they provide greater insight on the feasibility and merits of alternative policy options.

To assess the reliability of the data used in this study, we reviewed related documentation; conducted testing for missing data, outliers, and obvious errors; and traced data from source documents, where possible and appropriate. To the extent possible, we corroborated the results of our data analyses and interviews with other sources. In general, we chose databases that were commonly used by Treasury and researchers to monitor changes in federal debt and related transactions. To assess the reliability of the Google search data used in one of our cost models, we interviewed representatives from Google knowledgeable about the data and reviewed literature that made similar use of these data. To assess the reliability of the Bloomberg News Trends data used in our other cost model, we traced a sample of aggregate news story counts to their original publications. Based on our assessment, we believe that the data are reliable for the purposes described above.

See appendixes I and II for more details on our objectives, scope, and methodology.

We conducted this performance audit from June 2014 to July 2015 in accordance with generally accepted government auditing standards. Those standards require that we plan and perform the audit to obtain sufficient, appropriate evidence to provide a reasonable basis for our findings and conclusions based on our audit objectives. We believe that the evidence obtained provides a reasonable basis for our findings and conclusions based on our audit objectives.

BACKGROUND

Congress and the President first enacted statutory limits on federal debt during World War I to eliminate the need for Congress to approve each new debt issuance and provide Treasury with greater discretion over how it finances the government's day-to-day borrowing needs. With the Public Debt Act of 1941,[5] Congress and the President set a single overall limit on the amount of Treasury debt obligations that could be outstanding at any one time. Since then, Congress has passed and the President has signed more than 80 debt limit increases. Some were made after extensive congressional debate while others were not.

Federal debt subject to the limit includes both (1) debt held by the public and (2) debt held by government accounts (intragovernmental debt holdings).[6] The majority of debt held by the public consists of marketable Treasury securities, such as bills, notes, floating-rate notes, bonds, and Treasury Inflation-Protected Securities (TIPS), which are sold by Treasury through auctions and can generally be resold in a robust private sector secondary market by whoever owns them. Treasury also issues to the public a smaller amount of nonmarketable securities, such as savings securities, special securities for state and local governments, and government account series securities to deposit funds, such as the Government Securities Investment Fund (G Fund) of the Federal Employees' Retirement System. Debt held by the public primarily represents the amount the federal government has borrowed to finance cumulative cash deficits. Intragovernmental debt holdings represent balances of Treasury securities held in government accounts such as the Medicare and Social Security trust funds.

The debt limit does not control or limit the ability of the federal government to run deficits or federal agencies' ability to incur obligations. Rather, it is a limit on Treasury's ability to borrow to pay bills already incurred. Under current law, the decisions that create the need to borrow are made separately from—and generally earlier than—decisions about the debt limit. Nevertheless, increasing the debt limit frequently involves lengthy debate by Congress. Some argue that such debates surrounding the debt limit can raise awareness about the federal government's debt trajectory and also provide Congress with an opportunity to debate the fiscal policy decisions driving that trajectory. However, since this debate generally occurs after tax and spending decisions have been enacted into law and when debt is already at or near the limit, Congress has a much narrower range of options to effect an immediate change to fiscal policy decisions and hence to effect an immediate change to federal debt. Members of Congress have indicated interest in exploring alternatives to recent approaches to raising the debt limit by introducing more than 80 bills in the 112th and 113th Congresses to modify the process for changing the debt limit.

When federal debt is at the limit and delays in raising the debt limit occur, Treasury frequently has to depart from normal cash and debt management operations to avoid breaching the limit. Treasury refers to these actions as extraordinary measures. Treasury's normal cash management operations include ensuring that there is enough cash on hand to pay government obligations as they come due. To manage the federal government's day-to-day payments and receipts, Treasury holds cash in its operating cash balance in an account at the Federal Reserve.[7] Treasury can draw down its operating cash balance as debt approaches the limit, which allows Treasury to temporarily make payments without increasing the amount of debt subject to the limit.[8]

A number of extraordinary measures are available to Treasury to temporarily continue to manage debt if a delay in raising the debt limit should occur, but without a decision to raise the debt limit, they too run out. These measures reduce uncertainty over futures increases in debt subject to the limit (by suspending certain increases), or reduce the amount of debt subject to the limit. For example, Congress has authorized the Secretary of the Treasury (in certain situations) to redeem existing investments of the Civil Service Retirement and Disability Fund (CSRDF), and to suspend new investments to CSRDF in order to be able to continue to manage debt when it is at the limit.[9] Treasury also may suspend investments to the Government Securities Investment Fund of the Federal Employees' Retirement System (G-Fund), which contains contributions made by federal employees toward their retirement as part of the Thrift Savings Plan program. See appendix III for a table describing each of the extraordinary measures available to Treasury to manage debt when delays in raising the debt limit occur. Once all of the extraordinary measures are exhausted, Treasury may not issue debt without further action from Congress and could be forced to delay payments until sufficient funds become available and could eventually be forced to default on legal debt obligations.[10]

RECENT DEBT LIMIT INCREASES

On August 2, 2011, the President signed the Budget Control Act of 2011 (BCA), which provided for three increases in the debt limit that ultimately raised it to $16.394 trillion in January 2012,[11] ending a lengthy impasse over the debt limit in 2011.[12]

In February 2013, when debt was nearing the limit set in January 2012, the President signed the No Budget, No Pay Act of 2013, which suspended the debt limit until May 19, 2013.[13] The suspension was a new approach for adjusting the debt limit. Rather than set a dollar limit, under the suspension Treasury was allowed to borrow as necessary to fund obligations during the suspension period. When the limit was reinstated in May 2013, it was raised to an amount equal to the previous limit of $16.394 trillion plus the amount of qualifying debt incurred to fund obligations during the suspension period. This and subsequent laws provided that the debt limit would be increased by the amount of debt issued during the suspension period, excluding any issuance that is not necessary to make a payment that was required before the end of the suspension period. As a means of assuring itself that it has respected this limitation, Treasury has, toward the end of each suspension period, reduced its cash balance to approximately the level it was at on the date the suspension was enacted, regardless of cyclical or other cash management needs.

At the end of past suspension periods, the debt limit was reinstated at a level that required Treasury to immediately begin the use of extraordinary measures in order to borrow thereafter. Shortly prior to the reinstatement of the debt limit in May 2013, Treasury began using extraordinary measures to manage federal debt.[14] Debate over raising the debt limit continued into October 2013, when a lapse in appropriations required the federal government to shut down from October 1 until October 17.[15] During the shutdown, agencies without available funds were required to cease operations, except for activities excepted under the Antideficiency Act, such as activities necessary to protect from an imminent threat to life or property. On October 17, 2013, the President signed the Continuing Appropriations Act, 2014, which funded the government through until January 15, 2014, and suspended the debt limit again, this time through ending on February 7, 2014.[16] Figure 1 shows a timeline of key events leading up to the debt limit increase in October 2013. The debt limit was then suspended a third time, from February 15, 2014, through March 15, 2015.

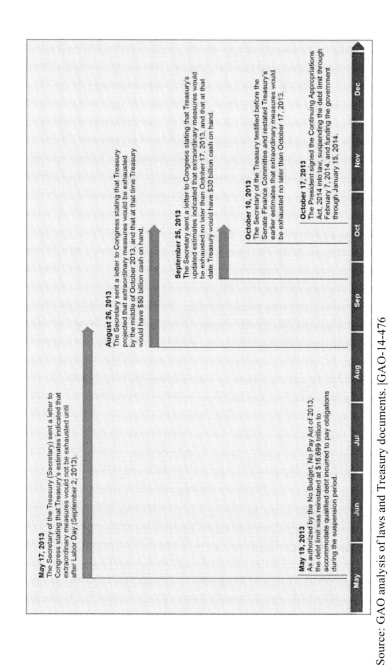

Source: GAO analysis of laws and Treasury documents. |GAO-14-476

Figure 1. Chronology of Events Leading Up to the Debt Limit Increase in October 2013.

At the conclusion of the most recent suspension on March 16, 2015, the statutory debt limit was reset such that debt subject to the limit was at the statutory limit of $18.113 trillion. Treasury began taking extraordinary measures in advance of that, beginning with the suspension of the sale of State and Local Government Series (SLGS) securities on March 13, 2015.

RECENT DEBT LIMIT IMPASSES DISRUPTED U.S. FINANCIAL MARKETS, AND INDUSTRY-LED CONTINGENCY PLANS TO ADDRESS A DELAYED PAYMENT WOULD NOT ELIMINATE SEVERE CONSEQUENCES

Market Participants Avoided Treasury Securities Due to Mature after Treasury Projected Extraordinary Measures Would be Exhausted

During recent debt limit impasses, investors reported systematically taking actions to avoid certain Treasury securities that matured around the dates when Treasury projected it would exhaust its extraordinary measures (at-risk Treasury securities), including selling them, not purchasing them, and not using or accepting them as collateral in financial transactions. These actions caused interest rates on at-risk Treasury securities to increase. They also caused a decline in liquidity for at-risk Treasury securities and ultimately added to Treasury's borrowing costs. Further, investors indicated that they are now prepared to take similar actions during future debt limit impasses. In addition to disruptions to the Treasury market and increased direct costs to Treasury, recent debt limit impasses also resulted in disruptions to other markets.

Disruptions in the financial sector due to the debt limit impasse could ultimately result in the increased costs for providing credit in the economy, either through increases in interest rates or in transaction costs. Consequently, lending in the economy may be reduced, and loans may become more costly. Reducing availability of capital may translate into lower levels of economic activity and growth. While it is difficult to quantify the cost increases arising from the 2013 impasse, they are nonetheless real and represent avoidable constriction in the provision of credit and growth in the economy.

Most of the market participants with whom we spoke said that they or their clients took action during recent debt limit impasses to avoid or minimize their holdings of Treasury securities, which were seen as most at risk of a delayed payment. Treasury securities are generally viewed as a highly liquid, safe haven asset and largely free of default risk. However, a number of market participants said that financial markets reevaluated the risks posed by the debt limit in the summer of 2011. This was in part due to unresolved questions about how a delayed payment from Treasury would be handled. In response, market participants began work on contingency plans. Those contingency plans generally were more fully developed and were implemented by the fall 2013 impasse. In at least one instance, the contingency plan included the unprecedented step of applying risk management tools normally reserved for more risky assets to Treasury securities. In 2013, investors acted quickly to target certain Treasury securities seen as most at risk during subsequent impasses.

Market participants we spoke with said that investors avoided holding hundreds of billions of dollars in Treasury bills with payments due in late-October through mid-November 2013. Market participants said that investors were primarily concerned with shorter-term Treasury bills that were maturing during this time. Some market participants told us that that notes and shorter-term bonds with interest payments due during this time were also affected, and some reported that they reviewed their holdings for such securities during this time and avoided purchases of those securities as well.

Table 1. Amount of Treasury Securities Considered by Some Investors to Be At-Risk Because of the 2013 Debt Limit Impasse, as of October 16, 2013 (in Millions of Dollars)

Date	Security Type	Amount Outstanding	Principal Due	Interest Due
10/17/13	Bills	119,994	119,994	
10/24/13	Bills	93,001	93,001	
10/31/13	Bills	89,000	89,000	
10/31/13	Notes/Bonds	773,300	61,395	5,886
Subtotal through the end of October 2013		**1,075,295**	**363,390**	**5,886**
11/7/13	Bills	83,998	83,998	
11/14/13	Bills	98,995	98,995	
11/15/13	Notes/Bonds	1,767,826	63,490	30,947
Total		**3,006,114**	**589,873**	**36,833**

Source: GAO analysis of Treasury data. | GAO-15-476
Note: Figures may not total due to rounding.

As table 1 shows, securities with principal payments due from mid-October through mid-November of 2013 represented nearly $600 billion, and those with either principal or interest represented more than $3 trillion in Treasury debt outstanding—about 25 percent of the debt held by the public at the time.[17] The institutions we spoke with had different approaches to managing their holdings of at-risk Treasury securities. Some institutions avoided these securities altogether, while others continued to buy and hold these securities but demanded higher yields on them than on other Treasury securities.[18]

Market participants we spoke with identified money market mutual funds as among the investors most affected by the debt limit impasse. All of the money market fund managers that we spoke with said that they had avoided at-risk Treasury securities during the 2011 or 2013 debt limit impasses or planned to do so during a future debt limit impasse. During the October 2013 debt limit impasse, five of the seven money market fund managers we spoke with reported either selling or avoiding purchases of the affected securities entirely. Some fund managers said they began changing their portfolios several weeks or months before the date on which Treasury was projected to exhaust extraordinary measures, before the broader market began to react to the debt limit impasse. Market participants told us that as substitutes for the at-risk Treasury securities, investors used bank deposits, agency discount notes—short-term securities issued by government sponsored enterprises (GSE) such as Fannie Mae, Freddie Mac, and the Federal Home Loan Banks—and commercial paper—short-term securities issued by corporations to raise cash needed for current transactions—as well as Treasury securities not seen as at risk.

Money market fund managers and other market participants cited a variety of reasons for selling at-risk Treasury securities. Money market fund managers and investors are relatively more risk averse and attempt to maintain stability in their portfolios, which is one reason that they invest in short-term, high quality securities, such as in Treasury bills. Securities and Exchange Commission regulations require most money market funds to maintain a stable value of a dollar per share, and the funds are therefore very sensitive to changes in the rates of securities in their funds, such as Treasury bills. Further, some investors seeking additional safety and stability can select money market funds that invest either primarily or exclusively in Treasury securities. Fund managers and other market participants said that Securities and Exchange Commission rules also contributed to their decision to avoid certain Treasury securities. These rules limit the ability of money market funds to hold defaulted securities without the approval of a fund's board of directors.[19] Several money market fund managers also told us that they spent a considerable amount of time and resources addressing client questions and concerns about their Treasury holdings and contingency plans in the event of a delayed payment. One fund manager who said they maintained their holdings of at-risk securities during the 2011 and 2013 impasses told us that they are unlikely to do so in a future impasse in order to address client concerns.

Broker-dealers we interviewed also reported limiting their exposure to the affected securities. According to statistics from the Federal Reserve Bank of New York, primary dealers' holdings of Treasury bills declined to as low as $16.2 billion on October 2, 2013, the lowest level of 2013 and less than half the average holdings of $39.3 billion for all of that year. [20] One broker-dealer who is not a primary dealer reported both not purchasing any affected securities and selling its entire holdings of them during the impasse.

Interest Rates Rose and Liquidity Decreased for At- Risk Treasury Bills that Investors Avoided During the 2013 Debt Limit Impasse

Investors' efforts to avoid shorter-term at-risk Treasury securities during the October 2013 debt limit impasse likely contributed to increases in interest rates and decreases in liquidity for Treasury bills in the secondary market—the market in which previously issued Treasury securities are bought and sold among investors. In 2013, secondary market yields on Treasury bills maturing in late October through mid-November rose from about 1 basis point (or one-one hundredth of a percent) in mid-September to over 50 basis points prior to the resolution of the impasse on October 17 (see figure 2). Rates in the secondary market ultimately affect Treasury's borrowing costs, as investors generally demand similar rates at auction to those in the secondary market. The significant increases in interest rates on these Treasury securities reflected a new level of investor uncertainty about Treasury's ability to pay its bills and avoid a delayed payment or a default.

Investors' efforts to avoid at-risk Treasury securities also likely contributed to changes in the volatility of rates on at-risk Treasury bills during the fall of 2013. For example, on October 8, 2013, the secondary market rate on the most recently issued 4-week Treasury bill increased 12 basis points— the largest one-day increase since March 2009. Similarly, on October 16, 2013, around the time the impasse was resolved, the rate on 1-month Treasury bills decreased by 21 basis points—the largest decrease since October 2008. Relatively large changes in Treasury rates, such as these, affect everyone from individuals, whose pension and money market funds invest in these securities, to global financial institutions, whose daily transactions in Treasury securities are vital to the U.S. and global financial markets.

Further, Treasury market participants we spoke with reported reduced liquidity—the ability to easily buy and sell securities in large volumes without meaningfully affecting the price—and reported instances of having difficulty trading those Treasury securities seen as at risk during the 2013 debt limit impasse. Bid-ask spreads—the difference between what price buyers are bidding on a security and what sellers are asking for that security, and a common indicator of market liquidity—increased on Treasury bills, with a larger spread indicating decreased liquidity. One market participant that we spoke with also reported that the reduced liquidity extended beyond those securities seen as at risk to other Treasury securities.

Treasury relies on high levels of liquidity to help fund the government at the lowest borrowing cost over time. Because the market for Treasury securities is highly liquid, Treasury avoids paying a significant liquidity premium—compensation to investors for the possibility that they might not be able to easily sell the security. A marked reduction in liquidity, even if temporary, could have serious long-lasting implications for the Treasury market, as it could affect the liquidity premium investors demand on Treasury securities.

Investors Did Not Accept At-Risk Treasury Securities as Collateral during the 2013 Debt Limit Impasse and Drove up Rates for Transactions Involving These Securities

Disruptions from the 2013 debt limit impasse extended to markets where Treasury securities are used as collateral. In many ways Treasury securities are the underpinning of the U.S. and global financial system, with Treasury securities being used in a broad range of financial transactions. However, financial institutions or their counterparties told us that during the impasse they did not accept certain Treasury securities as collateral in short-term financing arrangements, such as repurchase agreements, or other transactions, such as derivatives contracts.

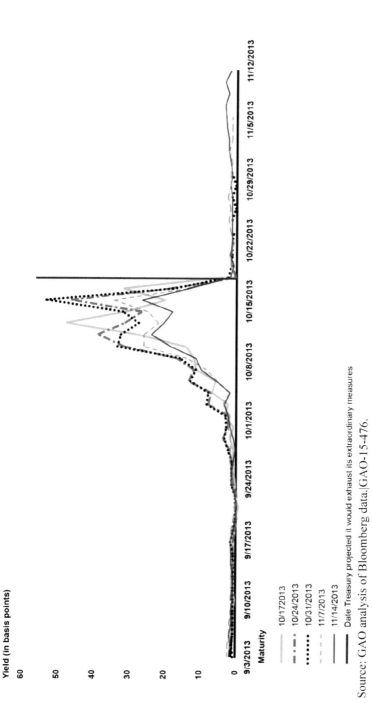

Source: GAO analysis of Bloomberg data.|GAO-15-476.

Figure 2. Secondary Market Yields on Treasury Bills Maturing in Late October through Mid-November 2013 (in Basis Points).

Treasury securities are one of the largest sources of high-quality collateral in the world. The ability to use Treasury securities widely as collateral at relatively low cost makes them easier to finance and more attractive to certain investors, including broker-dealers who borrow money in order to finance their holdings of Treasury and other securities. Because Treasury securities have historically been considered to be very low risk, they are among the lowest cost sources of collateral. Counterparties to financial transactions will often discount the value of collateral being provided based on several factors, including the perceived risk of the collateral (often known as a "haircut"), meaning that investors must provide more of any collateral if it receives a greater haircut. By using Treasury securities as collateral, counterparties may minimize the amount, and therefore the cost, of the collateral they must provide for a transaction. Given the low level of risk Treasury securities generally carry, the discount applied is generally lower than that applied to other types of collateral. Because the cost of collateral can be passed on to institutions and individuals that buy and sell securities or are engaged in other financial transactions, the use of Treasury securities as collateral lowers the cost for market participants. Recent debt limit impasses, however, have affected the treatment of Treasury securities as collateral. For example, one of the world's largest derivatives exchanges imposed a haircut on Treasury bills for the first time in 2011, in part due to the debt limit impasse.

Market participants told us that financial institutions avoided using certain Treasury securities as collateral by (1) informally requesting that their counterparties not deliver specific Treasury securities as collateral, (2) formally adjusting their list of acceptable collateral (or collateral schedules), or (3) avoiding investing or borrowing in the affected markets entirely. For example, managers of one of the world's largest derivative exchanges said that they requested their counterparties not to use Treasury securities with principal or interest payments due in mid-October through mid-November as collateral in derivatives contracts, and some market participants we spoke with reported that they or their counterparties on derivatives contracts and other agreements requested that different securities be substituted.

The market for repurchase agreements—or "repos"—is one market that relies heavily on the use of Treasury securities as collateral and that saw significant disruptions in recent debt limit impasses, including increases in rates. Under a repurchase agreement, an institution borrows funds from an investor using a security as collateral. For additional details on settlement and clearing arrangements for different types of repurchase agreements, see figure 3 below. Because the repurchase agreements are generally for very short periods, such as overnight, and the borrower provides collateral, borrowers generally are charged very low borrowing rates compared to other forms of borrowing. According to Federal Reserve data, as of October 9, 2013, almost 38 percent of tri-party repurchase agreements and 39 percent of General Collateral Finance (GCF) repurchase agreements in the United States were collateralized with Treasury securities.[21]

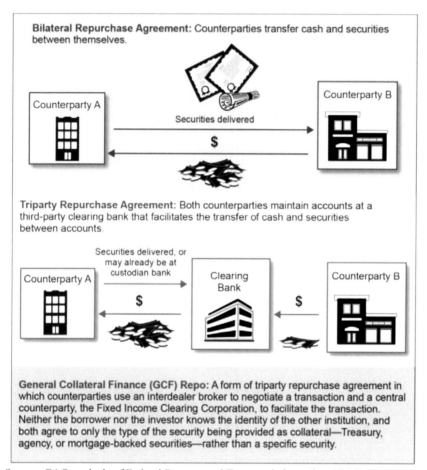

Source: GAO analysis of Federal Reserve and Treasury information. |GAO-15-476

Figure 3. Repurchase Agreement (Repo) Clearing and Settlement Arrangements.

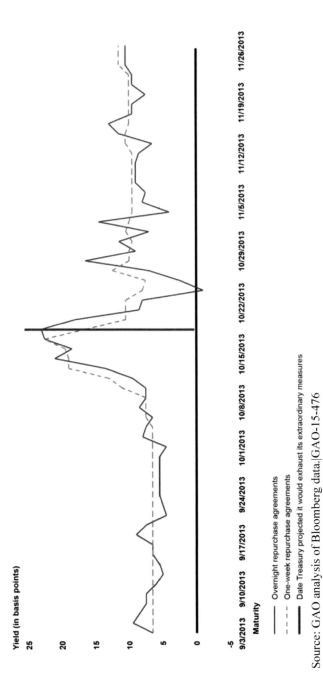

Source: GAO analysis of Bloomberg data.|GAO-15-476

Figure 4. Repurchase Agreement Yields, September 2013 to November 2013 (in Basis Points).

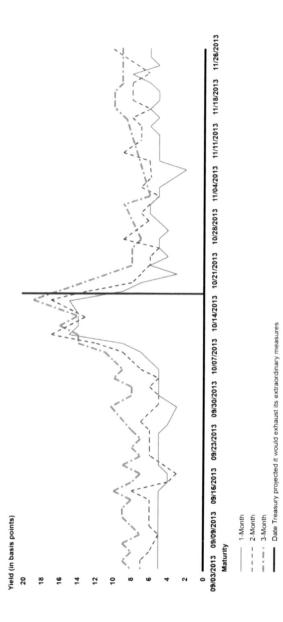

Source: GAO analysis of Federal Reserve data.|GAO-15-476

Figure 5. Non-financial Commercial Paper Rates, October 2013 to November 2013 (in Basis Points).

The market for repurchase agreements is critical to the health and stability of U.S. financial markets and the U.S. economy, as it serves as an important source of funding for broker-dealers that make markets in U.S. government and corporate securities. These broker-dealers make markets in government and corporate securities by matching buyers and sellers of securities or by buying and selling securities themselves. Broker-dealers fund their holdings of securities substantially through short-term borrowing, such as repurchase agreements. As of the end of 2013, repurchase agreements represented over half of the liabilities of broker-dealers. Higher short-term borrowing rates for these institutions may affect their ability to engage in market-making activities, ultimately resulting in lower levels of liquidity and higher borrowing costs for government and private borrowers.

Market participants we spoke with reported significant disruptions to the market for repurchase agreements during recent impasses, including increases in rates and the withdrawal of investors from the market. Because Treasury securities make up such a large portion of the collateral used in repurchase agreements, uncertainty about Treasury's ability to make payments on the government's obligations and avoid a delayed payment or a default likely affected this market, as investors had less certainty in the riskiness of the collateral being provided. As shown in figure 4, yields on overnight repurchase agreements—those that only last one day—increased more than 500 percent (from 4.5 basis points on September 30, 2013 to as high as 23 basis points on October 17, 2013). The two institutions that serve as clearing banks for tri-party repo transactions in the United States both told us that they received inquiries from clients about the ability to exclude certain Treasury securities from the list of acceptable collateral and that a few of their clients actually submitted such requests formally. One these institutions reported developing a template in 2013 to help facilitate this process of avoiding particular Treasury securities.

The Debt Limit Impasse Had Effects in Other Short-Term Markets

Recent debt limit impasses likely affected other short-term markets, including the market for commercial paper—short-term securities issued by corporations to raise cash needed for current transactions—and agency discount notes—short-term securities issued by GSEs such as Fannie Mae, Freddie Mac, and the Federal Home Loan Banks. Because Treasury securities often serve as a benchmark against which investors compare the returns on other products, increased rates on Treasury securities can lead to increased rates in other markets, affecting the borrowing costs of a range of borrowers. For example, during the 2013 debt limit impasse, the yield on 1-month commercial paper from financial institutions, such as banks, rose from 5 basis points on September 30, 2013, to 21 basis points on October 16, 2013; yields for other maturities and for non-financial issuers also saw increases. Figure 5 shows increases in rates on non-financial commercial paper. We used regression analysis to confirm that the rate increases for commercial paper were linked to the October 2013 debt limit impasse.

Further, yields on 3-month discount notes issued by the GSEs more than quadrupled from 3 basis points to 14 basis points between September 30, 2013, and October 16, 2013. Some market participants noted, however, that as significant as these increases in rates were, they were dampened by the fact that some investors invested in commercial paper or agency discount notes as an alternative to Treasury bills during the debt limit impasse, which caused rates in these markets to be lower than they otherwise might have been.

Market participants we spoke with also told us that some commercial paper issuers had delayed or otherwise changed issuance plans during the October 2013 debt limit impasse. Federal Reserve data is consistent with this observation. The amount of commercial paper outstanding issued by financial institutions declined each week from the week ending September 25, 2013, through the week ending October 16, 2013, indicating that less commercial paper was issued by financial institutions than matured during this time; the amount of commercial paper outstanding then rebounded the week after the debt limit impasse was resolved (see figure 6).[22]

Industry-Led Contingency Plans Address Some Uncertainty about How a Delayed Payment Would Be Handled but Would Not Eliminate the Severe Consequences of Such an Event

As described above, individual institutions took steps to manage risk related to debt limit impasses. In addition, financial sector industry groups led efforts to develop contingency plans in the event of a potential delayed Treasury payment, although they emphasized that the practices would only modestly reduce, not eliminate, the operational difficulties and potential damage posed by a delayed payment on Treasury debt. The industry groups stated that, even with these limited practices, a temporary delayed payment on

Treasury debt could undermine confidence in the full faith and credit of the United States and therefore cause significant damage to markets for Treasury securities and other assets, which would affect not only institutions but also individuals. Two sets of industry-led contingency plans are

- *A Treasury Market Practices Group (TMPG) white paper.*[23] Published in December 2013, this white paper was intended to provide a technical reference on some of the trading, clearing, settlement and other operational challenges that might arise in the unlikely event of a delayed payment on Treasury debt. Although this paper was not focused specifically on disruptions caused by a debt limit impasse, the paper laid out potential practices for how to manage a delayed payment on Treasury debt so as to modestly reduce, though not eliminate, the operational difficulties posed by the delay.[24] Under the proposed practice for principal payments, the group suggested that on the day before a payment is due, if Treasury determined that the next day's principal payment could not be made before the Fedwire Securities Service ran its end-of-day processes, Treasury could instruct the Federal Reserve Bank of New York to roll forward, or extend, the operational maturity date of the affected securities by one business day.[25] This would allow the security to remain transferable over the Fedwire Securities Service and could be repeated day by day until Treasury determined that the payment was able to be made. The paper also suggested practices for extending the coupon payment date for any interest payments that Treasury determined could not be made.
- *A Securities Industry and Financial Markets Association (SIFMA) contingency plan.* The SIFMA plan was developed for the financial industry's use in business continuity planning, along with a telephone call protocol that could be implemented among industry leaders on the night prior to an expected missed payment in order to facilitate communication and coordination among market participants.

Source: GAO analysis of Federal Reserve data.|GAO-15-476

Figure 6. Weekly Changes in Financial Commercial Paper Outstanding, September 2013 to November 2013 (Dollars in Billions).

Market participants told us that the two contingency planning efforts provided some reassurance about the continued ability to record, price, and transfer Treasury securities with a delayed payment. While these plans deal with technical and operational issues around a delayed payment, they do not reduce the consequences of a delayed payment. Even for the operational and technical issues, significant uncertainty remains about the implementation and effectiveness of these plans. This uncertainty includes

- *Sufficient advance notice.* One critical component of the potential practices described by TMPG and used in SIFMA planning is that Treasury would need to provide instructions to the Federal Reserve Bank of New York sufficiently in advance of the service's closing so that Federal Reserve officials have enough time to implement the extension of the operational payment date. Treasury officials with whom we spoke said that making the decision to roll forward or extend such dates in advance would be very difficult for Treasury as it could require a decision to be made while Congress is still debating legislation to raise the limit. Treasury did not provide input on the scenarios described in the TMPG paper. Treasury officials with whom we spoke said that any decision regarding Treasury's actions would be made based on the circumstances as they exist at that time. A Treasury official further stated that delaying payments could not reasonably protect the full faith and credit of the United States, the U.S. economy, or individual citizens from very serious financial harm.
- *Systems capabilities.* The extent to which private sector systems are able to accommodate a delayed payment is uncertain. For example, one primary dealer told us that the systems used for managing Treasury securities were designed separately from those used for managing other assets. According to market participants, because a delayed payment from Treasury was not an expected event, the systems for managing Treasury securities often were not set up to accommodate a delayed payment. Some with whom we spoke said that they had reviewed or tested their internal systems to determine whether they could handle a delayed payment. For some market participants, implementation of the strategy would require a great deal of manual intervention. Other participants said that they were hesitant to invest time and resources into making systems changes to prepare for an event that they believed to have a low probability of occurring.

Federal Reserve officials said that the Federal Reserve Banks, in their capacity as a fiscal agent for Treasury, tested their internal systems to determine if extending the operational maturity or interest payment date of a Treasury security would be feasible. Although they did find that their systems could handle such an approach, they emphasized that an additional challenge would be in managing the communications and logistics across public and private sectors necessary to implement a delayed payment. They also said that the conclusions of the TMPG paper should be revisited to make sure they are still valid in today's operating environment. When asked whether Treasury had tested the capabilities of its systems to delay payments, including principal, interest, and other payments, Treasury officials told us that no final decisions were made during the recent debt limit impasses and cautioned that any response would be entirely experimental and would create unacceptable risk to both domestic and global financial markets.

- *Questions about market response.* A number of market participants said that because securities considered in default are not acceptable as collateral for financial transactions, they were not sure whether a Treasury security on which a payment was delayed would still be considered acceptable collateral. In addition, market participants were uncertain whether Treasury would have, or would be provided with, the necessary legal authority to pay interest accrued on a delayed payment; this could have an impact on the willingness of market participants to buy and hold affected securities.

Beyond industry-led contingency plans, some market participants said that they assumed that, if necessary, Treasury would prioritize payment of principal and interest on debt held by the public over other federal payments. Treasury told us that no final decisions were made during the recent debt limit impasses. Treasury has explained publicly that— assuming Treasury has sufficient cash on hand—the Fedwire Securities System would technologically be capable of continuing to make principal and interest payments while Treasury was not making other kinds of payments, although this approach would be entirely experimental and would create unacceptable risk to both U.S. and global financial markets. One challenge would be that interest and principal payments on the relatively small share of securities purchased through TreasuryDirect—a platform for retail purchases of Treasury securities—do not go through the Fedwire Securities System.

Market Participants Expect to Use Similar Approaches in Future Impasses and Identified Factors that Could Make Impasses More Severe

Numerous factors can affect how the market responds to a debt limit impasse. For example, market participants noted that the 2011 debt limit impasse occurred at a time when the financial crisis in Europe was generally increasing demand for Treasury securities. At the same time, there was also uncertainty about how the 2011 debt limit impasse would affect the credit rating of the United States, including uncertainty about the full implications of a likely downgrade by one of the major rating agencies.[26] In general, market participants told us that financial markets were more prepared for the debt limit impasse that occurred in 2013. Market participants that we spoke with generally said that in any future debt limit impasses, they anticipated employing the same approach used in 2013, including systematically avoiding those Treasury securities that are seen as most at risk of a delayed payment. As described above, there can be market disruptions even if a payment delay does not actually occur, and these disruptions could potentially become more severe in the future as more market participants put contingency plans in place even earlier to avoid being the last one to react.

Further, market participants identified a number of other factors that could make a debt limit impasse more disruptive in the future. For example, market participants told us that the market reaction to the 2013 impasse was dampened because it occurred at a time when there was a very high level of demand and a shortage of supply for safe assets such as Treasury securities. According to some market participants, if alternative assets were more readily available to investors, the market reaction could have been much more severe, causing more disruption in the Treasury markets and exposing Treasury to additional increased funding costs. Another factor involves dealers' capacity to buy Treasury securities. Many market participants we spoke with, including both primary dealers and fund managers, noted that changes to market practices and new regulatory requirements, including new capital and liquidity requirements, are limiting dealers' ability and willingness to buy and hold securities during market disruptions such as a debt limit impasse. This potentially removes large buyers that traditionally have helped limit volatility and improve liquidity in Treasury markets during times of stress. Market participants stated that one reason that market reactions to future impasses may be more severe is that dealer capacity to buy Treasury securities is now more limited.

RECENT DEBT LIMIT IMPASSES RESULTED IN INCREASED BORROWING COSTS, DECREASED DEMAND FOR TREASURY SECURITIES, AND CONSTRAINED TREASURY CASH MANAGEMENT

Delays In Raising the Debt Limit in 2013 Increased Treasury's Costs, Particularly for Shorter Term Securities Auctioned in the Final Weeks of the Impasse

While increased rates on Treasury securities in the secondary market affect the amount of return on investment for investors, changes in the rates paid at Treasury auctions affect the amount that Treasury—and ultimately American taxpayers—pay in interest on federal debt. We used an econometric model to estimate the total increased borrowing costs incurred through September 30, 2014, on securities auctioned by Treasury during the 2013 debt limit impasse.[27] Overall, we estimated that these costs ranged from roughly $38 million to more than $70 million, depending on the specifications used.[28] The results of the models used in this report to estimate the additional borrowing costs to Treasury resulting from the 2013 debt limit impasse are not comparable to estimates for prior debt limit impasses published in past reports, which used different models.[29] See appendix II for a detailed description of the methodology we used to estimate increased borrowing costs.

The results of our analysis suggest that additional borrowing costs that Treasury incurred rose rapidly in the final weeks and days leading up to the October 2013 deadline when Treasury projected it would exhaust its extraordinary measures. Although our estimates suggest that modest cost increases began to appear in our model as early as February 2013, the estimated costs escalated rapidly at the very end of the impasse in 2013, with roughly 63 to 81 percent of the total estimated increase in borrowing costs coming from securities auctioned by Treasury in the final 10 days of the impasse—from October 7, 2013 to October 16, 2013. Roughly 33 to 64 percent of the increase in borrowing costs came from bills auctioned in the last two days of the impasse (see figure 7). Our estimates show increased borrowing costs on 26-week bills, for example, were over 23 times more on October 15, 2013 than they were at auction just one month earlier.[30]

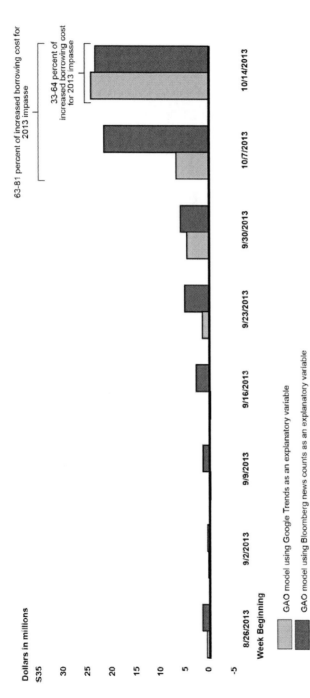

Source: GAO | GAO-15-476

Note: Our model also indicated smaller increased borrowing costs on securities issued prior to August 29, 2013 that are not shown here. The model regresses the difference between predicted and actual Treasury yields on one of two measures of public interest or concern over the debt limit impasse.

Figure 7. Estimated Increase in Borrowing Costs for Treasury Bills Auctioned Between August 26 and October 16, 2013 (Dollars in Millions).

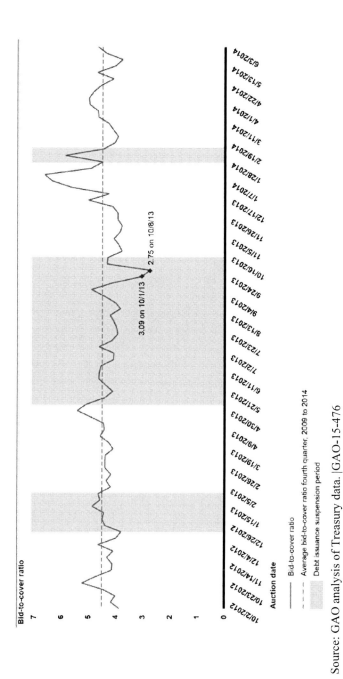

Source: GAO analysis of Treasury data. |GAO-15-476

Note: A debt issuance suspension period is a period in which, for the purposes of section 8348(j) of title 5, United States Code, Treasury determines that it cannot issue debt without exceeding the debt limit. Treasury must determine that a debt issuance suspension period exists and the length of the period in order to use certain extraordinary measures. See appendix III for more information on extraordinary measures.

Figure 8. Bid-to-Cover Ratio on 4-week bill auctions from October 2012 to June 2014.

Overall, most of the estimated increased borrowing costs were for shorter-term securities (or bills) with a maturity of 1-year or less. Interest rates on Treasury bills have been at historical lows in recent years, frequently auctioning at rates just a few hundredths of a percent—or basis points—above zero. While the additional interest costs attributable to the 2013 debt limit impasse were relatively modest compared to the overall face value of securities auctioned, in some cases they represented a significant share of the total interest due. For example, based on our models, several four-week bill auctions in September and October 2013 would have likely owed no interest had there been no debt limit impasse, but instead paid a total of approximately $11.8 million in interest.

ILLUSTRATIVE EXAMPLE OF EFFECTS OF THE DEBT LIMIT ON BORROWING COSTS AND DEMAND FOR TREASURY SECURITIES

Market concern over the delay in raising the debt limit can be seen through the comparison of two Treasury auctions for 5-day cash management bills held in the fall of 2013, both of which auctioned $35 billion of securities. The first auction was held on September 10, 2013 at a rate of 4 basis points—or 0.04 percentage points—and a bid-to-cover ratio of 3.77. The second auction was held a month later, on October 9, 2013— or approximately a week before Treasury was projected to exhaust extraordinary measures. In that auction, the auction rate increased to 30 basis points and the bid-to-cover dropped to 2.84, indicating both an increased cost and a decreased demand for Treasury securities at that time. If the rate for the October 9, 2013, cash management bill had been similar to the rate paid in early September, Treasury would have saved more than $1 million in interest.

This is intended to be an illustrative example. We did not control for other factors that can cause rates for Treasury bills to fluctuate from day to day, such as changes in the broader economy, as we did in our regression analyses.

Source: GAO-15-476.

The increase in borrowing costs for Treasury securities in October 2013 was accompanied by unusually low levels of demand for Treasury securities auctioned in the first weeks of October when concerns about the debt limit were at their highest. Demand for Treasury securities at auction can be seen in the bid-to-cover ratio, which is the dollar value of all bids received in the auction, divided by the dollar value of the securities auctioned. The bid-to-cover ratio for 13-week bills and 26-week bills were both well below the 5-year averages during the debt limit impasse in 2013, dropping to 3.13 and 3.52, respectively, at October 15 auctions. Similarly, at Treasury's 4-week bill auctions on October 1, 2013 and October 8, 2013, the bid-to-cover ratio was 3.09 and 2.75—the lowest levels since 2009 and below the 5-year average of 4.51 (see figure 8).

Debt Limit Restrictions Limit Treasury's Ability to Maintain Higher Cash Balances to Manage Unforeseen Risks

Debt limit restrictions can affect Treasury's ability to manage its operating cash balance, which can result in sharp declines in the amount of Treasury bills outstanding and limit Treasury's ability to manage unforeseen risks. The three laws enacted in the last 2 years that temporarily suspended the debt limit specified that following the suspension period, the limit was to be reinstated at a level equal to the previous level plus the amount of debt incurred during the suspension that was necessary to fund obligations that required payment during the suspension period.[31] Treasury was permitted to borrow the amount necessary to fund payments due during the suspension and in effect, the new amount of debt subject to the limit was deemed to be the new debt limit. However, as explained below, these laws have had the effect of altering Treasury's normal borrowing patterns.

In the normal course of events, Treasury's cash balance fluctuates due to changes in cyclical financing needs and changes in withdrawals and deposits. Under these laws, at the end of the suspension period the newly calculated debt limit has a limitation—it excludes any issuance that is not necessary to make a payment that was required before the end of the suspension period. As a means of assuring itself that it has respected this limitation, Treasury has, toward the end of each suspension period, reduced its cash balance to approximately the level it was at on the date the suspension was enacted. Therefore, these laws have had the effect of altering Treasury's normal borrowing patterns, contributing to sharp declines in Treasury's cash balance prior to the reinstatement of the debt limit. For example, in the weeks prior to the reinstatement of the debt limit, Treasury's cash balance declined from more than $200 billion on April 30, 2013, to roughly $34 billion on May 17, 2013. There was a similar reduction in Treasury's operating cash balance, from more than $121 billion on January 7, 2014, to roughly $34 billion on February 7, 2014, after another suspension ended and the debt limit was reinstated.

Treasury reduced cash in part by reducing the amount of Treasury bills outstanding, which can be disruptive to the markets in which Treasury transacts. Treasury typically makes adjustments to short-term borrowing needs by increasing or decreasing the amount of Treasury bills that it issues each week, rather than making adjustments to its schedule for notes and bonds, which can be more sensitive to changes in auction sizes. The reductions in Treasury's cash balance from April 30, 2013, to May 17, 2013, and from January 7, 2014 to February 7, 2014, were accompanied by reductions in the total amount of bills outstanding of roughly $92 billion and $114 billion, respectively.

OVERVIEW OF TREASURY CASH MANAGEMENT

Treasury maintains a cash balance to ensure that there is enough cash on hand to pay government obligations as they come due. Since Treasury disburses federal funds at federal agencies' request, it does not determine when such payments are made. The funds Treasury uses to make such payments come primarily from two sources: (1) tax revenues from sources such as personal and corporate income taxes, payroll withholdings, or other fees the federal government imposes; and (2) cash borrowed from the public through Treasury's regular auctions of debt securities.

Treasury must maintain an adequate cash balance in its account at the Federal Reserve to accommodate large swings in daily deposits and withdrawals. Treasury cannot risk an overdraft because the Federal Reserve is not authorized to lend to Treasury. Some large, regular payments and receipts—such as Medicare and Social Security payments and receipts from corporate taxes—cause meaningful swings in daily deposits and withdrawals, but many other payments and receipts can be more difficult to forecast.

Treasury's approach to cash management has changed since the financial crisis. Prior to 2008, Treasury generally targeted a $5 billion balance in its account at the Federal Reserve and held additional cash at authorized depositary institutions.

Treasury sought to maintain a balance in its account at the Federal Reserve large enough to protect against an overdraft under normal operating conditions. It also attempted to keep the cash balance stable to avoid interfering with the Federal Reserve's implementation of monetary policy.

Since the financial crisis, with short-term interest rates near zero, Treasury has maintained a significantly larger cash balance in its account at the Federal Reserve. In the past few years, Treasury also stopped holding additional cash at depository institutions but is not prevented from doing so again in the future.

Source: GAO-15-476.

These recent reductions in the amount of Treasury bills outstanding come at a time when demand for high quality liquid assets—such as Treasury bills—is high. In a presentation to Treasury, the Treasury Borrowing Advisory Committee—an advisory committee composed of senior representatives from investment funds and banks that meets regularly and provides recommendations to Treasury on a variety of technical debt management issues—attributed this high demand in part to recent regulatory changes. This includes increased capital and liquidity requirements stemming from provisions in the Dodd-Frank Wall Street Reform and Consumer Protection Act[32] and changes in bank capital rules. Financial institutions have met these requirements in part by increasing their holdings of Treasury securities. At the same time, Treasury bills as a share of total marketable debt have declined to historic lows in recent years as Treasury has extended the average maturity of federal debt, in part to manage rollover risk.[33] As of April 30, 2015, Treasury bills accounted for roughly 11 percent of marketable federal debt held by the public.

For a given demand, a reduction in the amount of Treasury bills outstanding is generally accompanied by a decline in short-term rates paid by Treasury and therefore lower borrowing costs for Treasury on those securities. However, Treasury officials and market participants stated that, in general, a large and irregular bill reduction over a short period of time has the potential to affect liquidity in the near term and also has the potential to add uncertainty and volatility in short-term rates over the longer term. Failure to timely raise the debt limit, including the requirement to return cash balances to pre-suspension levels, can affect Treasury's ability to adjust the amount of Treasury bills it auctions to react to changes in market dynamics.

Looking forward, debt limit constraints could also limit Treasury's recent efforts to maintain a larger cash balance to manage unforeseen risks. On May 6, 2015, Treasury announced changes to its cash management policy to better manage risks. Treasury stated that it would begin holding a level of cash generally sufficient to cover one week of outflows in its account at the Federal Reserve, subject to a minimum balance of roughly $150 billion. Treasury indicated that it intends to finance higher cash balances in part through increased issuance of Treasury bills. The decision to maintain higher cash balances was based on Treasury's own assessment of emerging threats, such as potential cyber-attacks, as well as a recommendation from the Treasury Borrowing Advisory Committee.

In August 2014, the committee recommended that Treasury maintain a higher cash balance to mitigate situations where normal access to funding markets through the auction of new debt may be disrupted or delayed. As examples, the committee noted that Treasury lost market access for 3 days following the September 11, 2001 attacks, for 1.5 days following Superstorm Sandy in October 2012, and for one day in December 2013, due to an issue with Treasury auction information technology. Based on analysis presented to the committee in August 2014, since 2009, a cash balance of roughly $330 billion would have been adequate to ensure that all government obligations could be met in the event that Treasury lost market access for up to 5 days. In comparison, Treasury's average operating cash balance for calendar year 2013 was less than $63 billion and peaked at $214 billion in April 2013.

We did not evaluate Treasury's specific proposed policy of maintaining a higher cash balance as part of this work. The benefits of maintaining a higher cash balance must be weighed against any potential costs associated with financing the higher balance. In general, managing cash balances at a prudent level is consistent with standards for internal control on responding to risk. Specifically, internal control standards state that management should design responses to the analyzed risks so that risks are within the defined tolerance for the defined objective.[34] In the past, Treasury and certain Federal Reserve banks, acting as fiscal agents for Treasury, have taken other actions to help manage operational risks related to Treasury debt management. For example, they added contingency sites that allow them to conduct auctions from alternative locations, if necessary. Decisions about how to finance a higher cash balance, given the stated benefits, should be consistent with Treasury's goal of achieving the lowest cost of borrowing over time.

As federal debt approaches the limit in the future, Treasury may need to reduce its cash balance in order to temporarily make payments without further increasing federal debt subject to the limit. As result, Treasury may be forced to deviate from its stated cash management goals and to maintain a lower cash balance than Treasury judges to be optimal for managing unforeseen risks, such as disruptions to normal market access. Market participants that we spoke with raised concerns that with a higher cash balance Treasury's actions to comply with future debt limit constraints could require an even steeper and more disruptive decrease in the supply of Treasury bills. This could add to volatility in the bill market, particularly if debt limit impasses occur frequently.

ALTERNATIVE APPROACHES TO DELEGATING BORROWING AUTHORITY THAT COULD MINIMIZE DISRUPTIONS IN THE TREASURY MARKET AND BETTER LINK POLICY DECISIONS WITH THEIR EFFECT ON DEBT

The debt limit was originally created to ease the process of borrowing to finance the operations of government. However, delays in raising the limit can lead to significant disruptions in the financial system and increased borrowing costs. The amount of debt necessary to comply with the statutes governing spending and revenue is a mathematical outcome of those spending and revenue amounts. Debates surrounding the debt limit may raise awareness about the federal government's current debt trajectory and also provide Congress with an opportunity to debate the fiscal policy decisions driving that trajectory. However, by the time the debt limit is reached and needs to be raised, Congress has a narrower range of options to effect an immediate change to fiscal policy decisions and hence to federal debt.

In previous reports we suggested that to improve its approach to delegating borrowing authority and to inform fiscal policy debate in a timely way, Congress should consider adopting a policy approach that both (1) minimizes disruptions to Treasury and financial markets and (2) better links decisions about the debt limit with decisions about spending and revenue at the time those decisions are made.[35] Based on our review of congressional testimony, legislation, input from budget and legislative experts, and our prior work, we identified three broad policy alternatives that met these criteria:

1) linking action on the debt limit to the budget resolution;
2) providing the administration with the authority to propose raises to the debt limit, subject to a congressional motion of disapproval; and
3) directly linking spending and revenue decisions to the debt limit by delegating broad authority to the administration to borrow as necessary to fund laws enacted by Congress and the President.

Each of these options maintains congressional control and oversight over federal borrowing. Each represents an approach that has in some form been proposed or actually used by Congress in the past. Each has strengths, weaknesses and design issues that members of Congress would need to consider. To assist in this consideration, we identified key design issues to consider for each option. These are based on discussions with policy and budget experts conducted via a closed web forum that we hosted in December 2014. In the forum, experts—including former congressional staff, academics, policy researchers, and other experts on congressional and budget processes— commented on the technical feasibility, design options, and overall merits of each of the alternatives.

Link Action on the Debt Limit to the Budget Resolution

Congress could link action on the debt limit to the concurrent budget resolution (budget resolution), which would better align decisions about fiscal policy with decisions about debt and would integrate debt limit decisions into the congressional budget process. Experts identified a number of advantages with this option. For example, it makes clear the relationship between spending and revenue decisions in the budget resolution and the debt implied by those decisions. Further, if there are concerns about the trajectory of future federal debt, it gives Congress the ability to take more immediate action to incorporate changes to revenue and spending at the time that Congress passes its annual budget plan, rather than waiting for the statutory debt limit to be reached. Related to this, it minimizes potential disruptions to the market by shifting the timing of the debate so that it occurs before debt is already at the limit.

OVERVIEW OF CONGRESSIONAL BUDGET RESOLUTIONS

The Congressional Budget and Impoundment Control Act of 1974, as amended, requires Congress to pass a concurrent budget resolution (budget resolution) each year on or before April 15 for the upcoming fiscal year starting October 1. A budget resolution establishes levels of spending and revenue for the upcoming year that reflects Congress' decisions regarding tax and expenditure policies, along with the amount of debt stemming from those decisions.

Specifically, budget resolutions set the appropriate levels for totals of new budget authority, outlays, and revenues; the surplus or deficit in the budget; and public debt for each upcoming fiscal year beginning on October 1 and for the 4 fiscal years thereafter. As a concurrent resolution, budget resolutions are adopted by both chambers of Congress but are not presented to the President for signature and therefore do not have the force of law. Meanwhile, changes to the debt limit must be passed as part of separate legislation, such as a bill or joint resolution.

Source: GAO-15-476.

Congress has previously recognized the link between the amount of federal debt and the spending and revenue decisions contained in the budget resolution through its rules and legislative procedures.

In past Congresses, the House rules provided that passage of a budget resolution automatically generated a joint resolution considered to have been passed in the House, changing the debt limit by the amount specified in the resolution.[36,37]

The Senate has not had a similar rule. It sometimes, though not always, has passed the joint resolution from the House, albeit with a lag and occasionally with added amendments. In the last 30 years, Congress has enacted debt limit increases that originated through this rule seven times—most recently in 2010.[38]

Design Issues to Be Considered

How should the debt limit be linked to the budget resolution and how would voting occur?

The debt limit could be linked to the budget resolution in one of two ways:

1. **The procedure previously used by the House to automatically change the debt limit could be used in both the House and the Senate.** The passage of the budget resolution by each chamber could automatically generate identical pieces of legislation changing the debt limit to the amount contained in the resolution. This legislation would be automatically deemed to have passed each chamber of Congress and would be immediately presented to the President for signature.

2. **Passage of a concurrent resolution on the budget in each chamber could generate legislation requiring a separate vote to raise the debt limit to the amount contained in the budget resolution.** To ensure that the debt limit and budget resolution are considered and debated in tandem, the legislation would be subject to expedited procedures, such as limits on the amount of debate and the ability to amend the legislation.

Both of these options could be achieved either through a modification to chamber rules or by amending the Congressional Budget and Impoundment Control Act of 1974. If implemented through chamber rules, it would have to be agreed to at the beginning of each Congress, since each Congress adopts its own rules. An amendment to the Congressional Budget Act would not require each Congress to revisit the decision.

Experts who favor an automatic change in the debt limit point out that the amount of debt stems directly from budgetary decisions, and since the budget resolution sets forth the budget for Congress, the two issues should not be separated. Meanwhile, experts who favor a separate vote on the debt limit suggest that this approach would help to increase transparency and further enhance members' awareness of how spending and revenue decisions affect federal debt. It would also minimize the likelihood that debate over the debt limit would prevent agreement and passage on a budget resolution. However, at the same time, a separate vote also makes it possible for Congress to adopt a budget resolution without changing the debt limit to the level dictated by that resolution.

Experts further identified factors that policymakers should consider when evaluating the option of linking action on the debt limit to the budget resolution.

Table 2. Comparison of Projected Debt Subject to the Limit in the Budget Resolution to the Actual Debt Subject to the Limit

Dollars in billions			
Fiscal year	Actual debt subject to the limit at the end of the fiscal year	Level of public debt or debt subject to the limit specified in the budget resolution	Difference(actual minus projected)
1995	4,884.6	4,965.1[a]	-80.5
1996	5,137.2	5,210.7[a]	-73.5
1997	5,327.6	5,435.7[a]	-108.1
1998	5,439.5	5,593.5[a]	-154.1
2000	5,591.6	5,628.4[a]	-36.8
2001	5,732.8	5,663.5[a]	69.3
2002	6,161.4	5,603.8[a]	557.6
2004	7,333.4	7,384.0[b]	-50.7
2006	8,420.3	8,645.0[b]	-224.7
2008	9,959.9	9,504.2[b]	455.7
2009	11,853.1	10,207.0[b]	1,646.1
2010	13,510.8	13,233.3[b]	277.6

Source: GAO analysis of legislation. | GAO-15-476

Notes: A concurrent budget resolution was not passed in fiscal years 1999, 2003, 2005, 2007 or 2011 to 2015.

[a] Represents the level of public debt specified in the concurrent resolution. A very small amount of public debt is not subject to the debt limit. This amount is primarily composed of unamortized discounts on Treasury bills and Zero Coupon Treasury bonds; debt securities issued by agencies other than Treasury, such as the Tennessee Valley Authority; and debt securities issued by the Federal Financing Bank. As of January 31, 2015, roughly 99.8 percent of public debt was subject to the debt limit.

[b] Represents the level of debt subject to the limit specified in the concurrent resolution.

How should this policy account for legislative and economic changes not included in the budget resolution?

Linking action on the debt limit to the budget resolution relies on accurate forecasting of projected debt levels, and may not account for unforeseen changes in tax revenue or mandatory spending that affect levels of debt. The actual amount of debt can differ from the amount anticipated in the budget resolution due to either (1) newly-enacted legislation, or (2) unanticipated fluctuations in the economy that affect the amount of revenue the government receives and the level of spending for certain programs, such as those that provide unemployment insurance or federal nutrition benefits without any explicit government action. Congressional response to such changes would vary depending on which type of change occurred.

As shown in table 2, during the 12 years in which Congress passed a budget resolution since 1995, actual debt subject to the limit exceeded the level of public debt or debt subject to the limit specified in the budget resolution for 5 of the years, by amounts ranging from $69 billion to $1.646 trillion. Actual debt was lower than projected debt in the other 7 years during that period, by amounts ranging from almost $37 billion to roughly $224 billion.

Legislative changes: Some experts proposed that the House and Senate modify their rules to require any legislation that changes the level of spending or revenue agreed to in the budget resolution to also include corresponding changes in the debt limit in order to accommodate the new level of debt.[39] This is similar to an approach that Congress took with three pieces of legislation enacted in 2008 and 2009 in response to the financial market crisis and economic downturn. The Housing and Economic Recovery Act of 2008, the Emergency Economic Stabilization Act of 2008, and the American Recovery and Reinvestment Act of 2009 (Recovery Act) each included a separate provision increasing the debt limit.[40] For example, in addition to spending and revenue provisions, the Recovery Act increased the debt limit by $789 billion, though federal debt at the time was more than $600 billion below the limit. This approach could be implemented either by enacting the requirement into law or by incorporating it into House and Senate rules.

Economic changes: In our previous report, we discussed additional options to deal with changes in debt driven by economic changes, such as: (1) considering further changes to the debt limit at the time that the annual mid-session review is released;[41] (2) setting aside a reserve fund in the budget resolution for unanticipated borrowing needs; and (3) delegating additional authority to Treasury to borrow for intrayear financing needs that resulted from changes in the economy rather than direct policy decisions.

What should be done in years in which Congress does not adopt a budget resolution?

The approach of linking action on the debt limit to the budget resolution works in years in which Congress passes a budget resolution. However, there are years in which Congress does not pass a budget resolution. For example, Congress has not passed a budget resolution for 9 of the 20 fiscal years since 1995. For such years, Congress would need to make any adjustments to the debt limit through an alternative process. One observer noted that in this event, the situation would be similar to what it is today—unless one of the other options was adopted as a backup procedure. Experts had different views on whether linking action on the debt limit to the budget resolution would make the passage of a budget resolution more or less likely to occur.

Provide the Administration with the Authority to Increase the Debt Limit, Subject to a Congressional Motion of Disapproval

Congress could provide the administration with the authority to propose a change in the debt limit, which would take effect absent adoption of a motion to disapprove by both the House and Senate. This is a variation of the approach contained in the Budget Control Act of 2011 (BCA), which gave the President the authority to propose two increases in the debt limit by such amounts and in such installments as specified in law. These increases would take effect unless Congress enacted a motion of disapproval in the form of a joint resolution within a specified number of days. A joint resolution requires a presidential signature and is subject to possible presidential veto. The BCA provided expedited procedures for the motion of disapproval in both chambers, including limits on debate and a prohibition on amendments. Congress could adopt legislation making this procedure permanent: providing the administration with ongoing authority to propose changes to the debt limit based on some criteria which would take effect absent adoption of a motion to disapprove by both House and Senate within a specified time frame.

Experts who favored such an approach noted that this would reduce the likelihood of market disruption and damage to the U.S. or world economy in part by changing the results of a lack of direct congressional action from a potential default to a debt limit increase. At the same time, it would preserve Congress's ability to debate fiscal policy decisions and the current trajectory of federal debt. Others believe it insufficiently links congressional decisions about spending and revenues from their impact on debt.

Design Issues to Be Considered

Should Congress specify criteria or require accompanying explanatory information for proposed debt limit increases? If so, what should they be?

To align the timing of the debt limit modification with the budget process, the amount of proposed changes to the debt limit could be tied to specific projections of federal debt in the congressional budget resolution, the President's budget, or recently enacted legislation, as suggested in pieces of previously introduced legislation. This would strengthen the link between decisions about spending and revenue and decisions about debt.

Under the BCA, the President had the authority to propose increases when debt came within $100 billion of the limit. Some experts suggested that changes to the debt limit could instead be proposed and considered on a key date selected from the congressional calendar, rather than when debt subject to the limit reached a certain dollar amount. This would enable Congress to align the timing of action on the debt limit with the budget process or other congressional decision making.

How should Congress structure the vote of disapproval?

BCA provided one model for structuring the votes of disapproval. Congress could consider alternative approaches and structural decisions, such as how much time will be afforded to pass a motion of disapproval before the change takes effect. Under BCA, first, a portion of a debt limit increase was not to take effect if a joint resolution of disapproval was enacted into law within 50 calendar days after Congress received the President's formal notification that additional borrowing was required to meet existing commitments in the first instance. Then for a second debt limit increase, all of the increase was not to take effect if such a joint resolution was enacted into law within 15 calendar days.

Directly Linking Spending and Revenue Decisions to the Debt Limit by Delegating Broad Authority to the Administration to Borrow As Necessary to Fund Enacted Laws

Congress could adopt the approach similar to the one used in some other countries: delegate to the administration the authority to borrow such sums as necessary to fund implementation of the laws duly enacted by Congress and the President. This would minimize disruptions in Treasury's debt and cash management and would remove the dangers that accompany fear of default by the U.S. government. Since laws that create the need for debt require adoption by the Congress, this would maintain congressional control over the amount of federal borrowing necessary. The recent approach of suspending the debt limit and permitting Treasury to borrow the sums necessary to meet obligations is a short-term version of this option, in which the Treasury is authorized to borrow as necessary to fund obligations incurred by the government until the date on which the limit is reinstated. As we previously reported, providing finance departments with broad authority to borrow is consistent with practices in certain foreign countries.[42] In the United Kingdom, for example, the Treasury is given broad authority to raise money in a manner it "considers expedient for the purpose of promoting sound monetary conditions." In New Zealand, the Minister of Finance is given similarly broad borrowing authority.

Some of the experts with whom we spoke found the lack of a specific nominal debt limit to be a positive feature of this approach since it permitted responses to changes in the economy and legislation. Others saw this as offering too little focus on the link between spending and revenue decisions and the level of debt incurred. To improve the transparency surrounding the state of public finances under this approach, Congress could consider requiring additional reporting from Treasury when debt limit modifications are proposed. For example, some experts suggested that reports delineating the specific sources for changes in federal debt, such as the laws passed during the year, or the state of public finances in general, could be beneficial in tandem with this policy. When the Australian parliament repealed its debt limit in 2013, it required the government to provide information regarding the amount and types of debt outstanding, as well as reasons for any substantial unforeseen increases in debt beyond a certain threshold.

Design Issues to Be Considered

What form should congressional oversight of Treasury debt management take in light of this delegation of authority? What reports might be required from Treasury and at what frequency?

This option seeks to recognize that the amount of borrowing is a function of previously enacted spending and revenue laws. It eliminates the threat of a possible default and the disruptions that fears of default create. However, for those who believe that the debt limit provides a focal point for changes in the fiscal policy path or for discussion and debate over spending and revenue, this approach offers little unless it is accompanied by additional provisions.

Some countries require an annual report by their treasury or department of finance ministry on debt and debt management. Such a report could cover several major areas, including the demand for different types of Treasury securities, information on who holds U.S. Treasury securities, information on the major drivers of changes in borrowing during a specified period, and projections and possible scenarios for near-, medium-, and long-term borrowing needs.

Replace the After-the-Fact Debt Limit with a Fiscal Rule Imposed on Spending and Revenue Decisions

Experts had differing views on the effectiveness of the current debt limit on controlling growth in the federal debt. Some pointed to the fact that debt limit increases were accompanied by legislation enacting budget controls as evidence of their usefulness to control spending. For example, debt limit increases were enacted as part of legislation that included budget controls seven times between 1985 and 2014.[43] Others point to the mixed results from these laws. Regardless of how experts view the current debt limit, many shared a concern that the federal government's current fiscal path is unsustainable. To address this concern, some experts supported replacing the after-the-fact debt limit with a fiscal rule imposed on spending and revenue decisions. A number of individuals and groups have proposed using debt or debt targets as a fiscal rule that binds decisions on spending and revenue. One such proposal was for a rule that would go beyond "PAYGO," the statutory pay-as-you-go requirement to generally offset the aggregate effect of increases in mandatory spending or reductions in revenue. Under the debt version, Congress would agree on a declining path for debt as a share of gross domestic product (GDP);

legislation would be measured against this path. Other proposals use different targets and enforcement mechanisms.

Policymakers Could Consider Combining the Different Approaches

Policymakers could consider combining the different approaches described above. For example, the option of tying the debt limit to the budget resolution offers the advantage of explicitly linking the debt limit to the congressional plan for spending and revenue. It does not, however, provide for increases in debt that result from economic downturns. Further, this approach would not provide for increases made necessary by subsequent legislation unless Congress required any legislation that would increase debt beyond that assumed in the resolution to include a commensurate increase in the debt limit (as with the Recovery Act, for example). To deal with this contingency—and for situations in which no concurrent resolution on the budget is adopted—Congress might wish to combine this option with the one that permits the President to propose an increase that would take effect absent a congressional motion of disapproval. Any of the options for changing how the debt limit is adjusted and set could be combined with adoption of a fiscal rule aimed at reversing the current path for debt as a share of GDP. Any of them could also be accompanied by requirements for reports from Treasury that would assist Congress in its oversight of debt management.

CONCLUSION

Treasury securities play a critical role in the world's economic and financial system. The confidence investors have that debt backed by the full faith and credit of the United States will be honored offers the nation and its taxpayers many benefits, including lower interest costs on our debt. Recent changes in how financial institutions view the risk of a delayed payment on a Treasury security and how they manage those risks raise serious concerns. Unlike debt limit impasses during earlier years, financial institutions now have processes and systems in place to make very rapid adjustments to their holdings of Treasury securities, including widespread avoidance of large amounts of Treasury's debt. As a result, the effects of the debt limit on financial markets in the future could be more sudden and severe, giving Treasury and policymakers less time to react.

Congress's recent approach of suspending the debt limit until a specified date did eliminate one source of uncertainty—the date when federal debt will hit the statutory limit when Treasury will need to begin using extraordinary measures to avoid breaching the limit. However, this additional certainty came at a cost to Treasury's cash management. Treasury is required to maintain a sufficient cash balance to pay obligations as they become due. Treasury makes payments at federal agencies' request; it does not control the timing of these payments. At the end of past debt limit suspensions, Treasury sharply reduced its cash balance to match the cash that it had on hand just prior to each suspension to ensure that it complied with legal limitations. This can be disruptive to the financial markets that Treasury relies on to issue debt, and limited Treasury's flexibility to make decisions about the appropriate level of its cash balance. The level of Treasury's cash balance should be flexible and based on the federal government's immediate borrowing needs, evolving market conditions, and current assessment of perceived risks.

The current after-the-fact approach to the debt limit does not tie decisions about the level of debt to the decisions about spending and revenue at the time those decisions—which are a major determinant of the level of debt—are made. There are approaches to the debt limit that would make that link stronger by having Congress consider the impact of budget decisions on the amount of debt at the time it makes decisions about spending and revenue. This kind of process would also improve the public understanding of this link and perhaps facilitate more informed discussion about the steps necessary to slow the increase in federal debt. We examined several suggested approaches, and based on interviews with knowledgeable budget and legislative experts and a closed web- based forum, offer three main alternatives for consideration. All of them would mitigate market disruption, permit improved cash management at Treasury, and tie the debt limit to spending and revenue decisions at the time those decisions are made.

MATTERS FOR CONGRESSIONAL CONSIDERATION

To avoid serious disruptions to the Treasury market and to help inform the fiscal policy debate in a timely way, Congress should consider alternative approaches that better link decisions about the debt limit with decisions about spending and revenue at the time those decisions are made such as those described in this report. However, if Congress chooses to continue to temporarily suspend the debt limit, it should consider providing Treasury with more flexibility in the level of Treasury's operating cash so that it is based not on the level that it was just prior to a suspension period, but on the federal government's immediate borrowing needs. This would minimize some of the disruptions to Treasury's normal cash management and debt issuance.

AGENCY COMMENTS

We requested comments on a draft of this report from the Secretary of the Treasury and the Chair of the Federal Reserve System. On June 11, 2014, the Deputy Assistant Secretary for Federal Finance provided us with the comments via e-mail, indicating that Treasury agreed with the findings in the report regarding primary and secondary market functioning during the 2013 debt limit impasse. Treasury stated that the findings corroborate Treasury's observations as well as market color and commentary that Treasury received from market participants. Treasury also agreed that "the current congressional method for dealing with the debt ceiling is clearly sub-optimal." Treasury stated that it "sees advantages to GAO's recommendations for improvements around the debt limit process and would like to see more details" regarding each of the proposals discussed.

Both Treasury and the Federal Reserve System provided technical comments, which we incorporated as appropriate.

Susan J. Irving
Director for Federal Budget Analysis
Strategic Issues

APPENDIX I: OBJECTIVE, SCOPE, AND METHODOLOGY

The objectives of this report were to examine the effect of delays in raising the debt limit in 2013 on (1) the broader financial system and (2) Department of the Treasury (Treasury) debt and cash management and (3) to examine alternative approaches to delegating borrowing authority that would tie decisions about the debt limit to the spending and revenue decisions that lead to debt and also could minimize future disruptions in the Treasury market.

To examine the effects of the debt limit on financial markets, we interviewed more than two dozen private sector market participants and observers to obtain their views and to learn about any contingency plans they developed. We also interviewed Treasury officials and Federal Reserve staff. We selected market participants to ensure a diversity of viewpoints, taking into consideration market sector, share of the Treasury market, and recommendations of market experts. Interviewees outside the Treasury and the Federal Reserve were representatives from six primary dealers, three commercial banks, seven money market mutual funds and bond funds, three clearing banks, the three largest rating agencies in the United States, a private asset manager, managers of one of the world's largest derivative exchanges, and a widely recognized expert and commentator on the Treasury market. The views expressed in these interviews are not generalizable to all market participants.

To further assess the effect of the October 2013 debt limit impasse on secondary markets for Treasury securities and on markets for private securities, we analyzed data on rates for Treasury securities in the secondary market, repurchase agreements, and nonfinancial commercial paper, and data on the amount of financial commercial paper outstanding obtained from the Federal Reserve and Bloomberg for the period from September 2013 to February 2014. We compared this data to key dates related to the debt limit to identify noticeable changes in market conditions around the time of the debt limit impasse. We used publicly available data, including data from Treasury's Monthly Statement of Public Debt and Daily Treasury Statement to calculate the amount of principal and interest on Treasury securities that was due from October 17, 2013, to November 15, 2013.

To estimate the immediate effect of the debt limit impasse in October 2013 on the borrowing costs paid by Treasury, we used econometric models to produce estimates of the increased interest demanded by the markets for Treasury securities. The models used indicators of the evolving perception of the risk of disruptions in Treasury payments to estimate daily yield premiums associated with the rapid escalation in market concern over the final days and weeks of the impasse. For these indicators of concern, we used (1) daily data on searches of terms related to the debt limit impasse obtained from Google for the period from February 5, 2013, to October 16, 2013, and (2) daily counts of news articles that used terms related to the debt limit impasse obtained from Bloomberg for the same period. We then applied the resulting estimates of increases to interest costs attributable to the debt limit to Treasury auctions held during the relevant periods to estimate the direct costs incurred by Treasury through September 30, 2014. For this part of the analysis, we used daily data on Treasury auctions for the period from February 5, 2013, to October 16, 2013. For additional information about the modeling and cost analysis, see appendix II. This analysis is not designed to capture long term costs associated with market perceptions of an increased political risk associated with Treasury securities.

To further assess the effect of recent debt limit impasses on Treasury debt and cash management, we used data on the results for Treasury auctions from 2009 to 2014 downloaded from Treasury's website and analyzed changes in demand for Treasury securities. Older data from 2009 to 2012 were used to analyze historical trends prior to the debt limit impasses. We also reviewed publicly available data on Treasury's operating cash balance from Daily Treasury Statements from October 2010 to February 2014. We compared this to data on the total amount of Treasury bills outstanding during this period. We also reviewed press releases, presentations, and meeting minutes of the Treasury Borrowing Advisory Committee.

To identify and examine alternative approaches to delegating borrowing authority, we interviewed budget and legislative experts including former congressional staff, former Congressional Budget Office (CBO) directors and Office of Management and Budget (OMB) staff, and other congressional observers from a range of policy research organizations that represented a wide range of political views. We also reviewed all legislation pertaining to the debt limit introduced in the 112th and 113th Congresses, as well as congressional testimony on the debt limit since 2011. Based on the interviews and analysis as well as our previous work on the debt limit, we identified three policy options that could potentially minimize disruptions in the Treasury market and that link decisions about debt to decisions about spending and revenue.

To obtain greater insight on these policy options, we hosted a private web forum where selected experts participated in an interactive discussion on the various policy proposals and commented on the technical feasibility and merits of each option. We selected experts to invite to the forum based on their experience with budget and debt issues in various capacities (government officials, former congressional staff, and policy researchers), as well as on their knowledge of the debt limit, as demonstrated through published articles and congressional testimony since 2011. We also sought to include a range of political perspectives by taking into consideration factors such as an expert's past political appointments. The forum was open to participants from December 1 to 15, 2014, and we received comments from 17 of the 55 experts invited to the forum. The other experts were not reachable or were unable to participate in the time frames that we provided. The 17 that did participate represented a wide range of political views, consistent with the entire list of those invited. We analyzed the results of the forum to identify key factors that policymakers should consider when evaluating different policy options. Although these results are not generalizable to all experts with relevant expertise, they provide greater insight on the feasibility and merits of alternative policy options.

To assess the reliability of the data used in this study, we reviewed related documentation, conducted testing for missing data, outliers, obvious errors, and traced data from source documents, where possible and appropriate. To the extent possible, we also corroborated the results of our data analyses and interviews with other sources. In general, we chose databases that were commonly used by Treasury and researchers to monitor changes in federal debt and related transactions. To assess the reliability of Google search data used in one of our cost models, we interviewed representatives from Google knowledgeable about the data and reviewed literature that made similar use of these data. To assess the reliability of Bloomberg News Trends data used in an alternative model, we traced a sample of aggregate news story counts to their original publications. Based on our assessment, we believe that the data are reliable for the purposes described above.

We conducted this performance audit from June 2014 to July 2015 in accordance with generally accepted government auditing standards. Those standards require that we plan and perform the audit to obtain sufficient, appropriate evidence to provide a reasonable basis for our findings and conclusions based on our audit objectives. We believe that the evidence obtained provides a reasonable basis for our findings and conclusions based on our audit objectives.

APPENDIX II: DETAILED METHODOLOGY AND FINDINGS OF STATISTICAL ANALYSIS OF TREASURY BORROWING COSTS NEAR THE DEBT LIMIT

To estimate the immediate effect of delays in raising the debt limit in October 2013 on the Department of the Treasury (Treasury) borrowing costs, we developed a suite of econometric models. The models resulted in estimates of increased interest rates, which we applied to Treasury auctions held during the relevant period to arrive at an estimate for the direct costs to Treasury from the debt limit impasse. Market participants told us that additional interest was demanded to compensate for both the risk of a potential disruption in principal and interest payments stemming from the impasses and for any liquidity effects affecting the ability to buy and sell Treasury securities in large quantities without influencing the price. According to market participants, liquidity effects were due in part to some market participants refusing to buy certain securities in anticipation of a potential disruption.

Our econometric models use time series analysis, a standard approach used in financial econometrics when analyzing asset prices over time. One reason time series models are preferred in financial asset price modeling is that the structure of a time series model parallels that of the weak version of the Efficient Market Hypothesis, which states that risk-adjusted asset prices incorporate all public information that are relevant to the price of the asset. This suggests that yesterday's prices incorporate all economic fundamental information and will do so more flexibly and accurately than any econometric model specification that tries to control explicitly for economic fundamentals.

The results of the models used in this report to estimate the additional borrowing costs to Treasury resulting from the 2013 debt limit impasse are not comparable to estimates for prior debt limit impasses published in past reports, which used different models.[44] The approach that we used in this report offered us a number of advantages. Most notably, for 2013 it allowed us to model the escalation of the impasse on a day-by-day, auction-by-auction basis. With this modeling approach, we were able to capture the rapid increases in Treasury yields in the days and weeks before Congress and the President resolved the impasse by suspending the debt limit. In general, market participants told us that the debt limit impasse in 2011 affected markets more broadly but effects were concentrated over a short period of time. In contrast, the effects of the 2013 debt limit impasse were more targeted to specific securities and appeared earlier, in part because of the contingency planning discussed in the report. These and other market differences were described to us by participants. In this report we do not establish a causal link between individual factors that contribute to the differences between each debt limit impasse and their effects on Treasury's borrowing costs.

Modeling Approach Used for This Report

We took a three-step approach to modeling Treasury's borrowing costs attributable to the debt limit impasse resolved in October 2013.

1. We identified suitable benchmark securities for each Treasury maturity that (1) had a demonstrated statistical relationship with the Treasury security prior to the most evident market response to the impasse, and (2) did not show evidence of spillover effects.[45] Using the benchmarks to predict Treasury yields in the absence of a debt limit impasse, we estimated the daily deviation of predicted Treasury yields from actual Treasury yields (using the Constant Maturity Treasury daily series) for the period of February 5, 2013, to October 16, 2013. This step helped us control for movements in yields unrelated to the debt limit impasse during the time period under consideration.

2. Using the series of error terms estimated in the first step of the analysis as the dependent variable, we fit regression models with each of two proxies for market concern over the debt limit impasse as an explanatory variable and a full set of appropriate time-series lags in the mean and variance terms to control for the autoregressive characteristics of the data. In this step we estimated a daily cost premium, in percentage points, associated with the debt limit impasse.

3. In the final step of the analysis, we used the estimated cost premiums associated with the relevant Treasury maturity and date and applied these premiums to Treasury auction data to estimate a total per auction cost attributable to the debt limit impasse.

We selected eight economists with relevant expertise to review our econometric approach and assess its strengths and limitations and received comments from the five that were available to participate in our study. The other three were not available to participate in our study. Those that responded agreed with our general approach and provided technical comments for us to consider. To address these comments, we either modified our econometric approach or disclosed additional limitations of our approach, as discussed below. Before selecting these experts, we reviewed potential sources of conflicts of interest, and we determined that the experts we selected did not have any material conflicts of interest for the purpose of reviewing our work.

Proxies for Market Concern Over Debt Limit Impasse

Visual inspection of Treasury data and our interviews with market participants indicated that concern over the potential for market disruption escalated rapidly over the final days and weeks of the impasse. The rapid escalation that we observed in Treasury yields is what we term the "acute" period of the impasse and is the main source of costs our models are designed to identify. We identified two measures that proxy for the timing, pace, and severity of the escalation of that concern: Google Trends data and Bloomberg News Trends series counts of news articles that contain key phrases. See figure 9 for an illustration of the Treasury yield dynamics and the proxy dynamics.

The Google Trends data is a measure of the frequency of searches on Google for various phrases, provided by Google. In our case, the phrases of interest in our searches all relate to the debt limit. Google Trends data has been used successfully in other private sector and public sector studies to capture changes in public interest in an issue.[46] A potential limitation is that this measure captures the general public's interest over the debt limit, which might vary in systematic ways from the interest of market participants and institutions whose decisions affect prices.

We requested daily data from Google on searches for the following five terms: debt ceiling, U.S. debt ceiling, U.S. debt crisis, debt limit, and U.S. default. Google provided us with daily data on these five terms for the period January 2010 – September 2014. Older data was used to establish historical trends prior to the debt limit impasses. The data provided by Google has been normalized by the company in order to protect the privacy of searches in low volume environments by dividing each day's search volume by the volume of the first day included in the data. The normalization procedure complicates our ability to compare volumes across search terms. To accommodate the effects of the normalization and to combine the data into one measure, we conducted a principal components analysis to extract the principal factor as our measure. The principal factor accounts for almost 97 percent of the variance across the terms, indicating that the five terms do capture a unified construct. Our final measure is a linear shift of the principal factor so that there are no negative values of the measure.

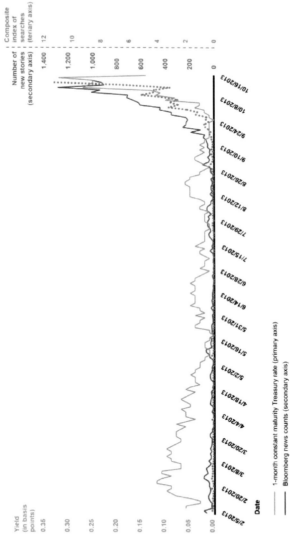

Source: GAO analysis of Treasury, Bloomberg News Trends, and Google Trends data. | GAO-15-476

Note: Constant Maturity Treasury rates are calculated by Treasury based on the yield on a security to its time to maturity and the closing market bid yields on actively traded Treasury securities in the over-the-counter market. This method provides a yield for a 1-month maturity, even if no outstanding security has exactly 1 month remaining to maturity.

Figure 9. Rise in Constant Maturity Rate for One-Month Treasury Securities and Corresponding Rise in Proxy Measures of Interest in the Debt Limit, from February 5, 2013, to October 16, 2013.

The Bloomberg News Trends data counts the number of news articles that mentioned either "debt limit" or "debt ceiling" or both.[47] This is another commonly used type of measure to capture public concern over an issue. This series has the advantage of drawing from the some of the same sources that populate the news tickers on Bloomberg terminals for traders and other market participants who have chosen to follow the debt limit standoff. It therefore has a direct relationship with the materials that are likely to be contributing to market participants' risk assessments. On the other hand, the news stories are produced at a much smaller volume than are Google searches and they reflect the judgment of a comparatively small number of people (i.e. the journalists and editors that produce the stories) about how newsworthy the issue is.

Both the Google data series and the Bloomberg News Trends data series that we created have similar dynamics and show clear spikes around the time of each debt limit impasse in the last four years.

Identification of Benchmarks

Including an appropriate benchmark security in a model helps control for movements in rates that are due to market dynamics not related to the debt limit impasse. In order to be considered appropriate, a benchmark security needs to have, in normal times, a reliable equilibrium relationship with the target Treasury security. In addition, however, it needs to not suffer from spillover effects due to the debt limit impasse—the candidate benchmark would not serve its function if it too had substantial price movements resulting from the debt limit impasse.

We considered several candidate series as benchmarks. For bills (through 1-year maturities), we tested the following:

- Federal Funds Rate Data (Fed Funds)
- London Interbank Offered Rate (LIBOR) (overnight, 1- , 3- , 6-month, and 1-year maturities)
- Financial Commercial Paper (1- , 2- , 3-month maturities)
- Non-financial Commercial Paper (1- , 2- , 3-month maturities)
- Eurodollar Rates (1- , 3- , 6-month maturities)

For notes, bonds and the 1-year bill, we tested swap rates with 1- , 2- , 3-, 5- , 7-, 10-, and 30-year maturities.

We tested the two criteria for our benchmarks separately. First, we eliminated candidates that suffered spillover effects in the acute period of the impasse. Then we tested each remaining candidate against each Treasury for equilibrium relationships during the non-acute period of the data.

In order to isolate a time period prior to major market disruptions due to the debt limit event that would allow us to test the appropriateness of benchmarks in the relevant time frame, we used both the Google Trends data and the Bloomberg New Trends counts data to identify when interest in the debt limit started to increase. We used a simple algorithm to identify possible cutoff dates for the non-acute period. Our algorithm identified dates that met the following criteria:

1. Count on that date was higher than all others, beginning a week after the resolution of the previous debt limit impasse.
2. The previous day also did not meet the criteria.

This algorithm produced three candidate dates common to both data sets, and we selected the first of these, August 27; therefore defining the non- acute period of the impasse as running from February 5, 2013 through August 27, 2013, and the acute period as running from August 28, 2013, through October 16, 2013. We ended our window the day before the impasse's resolution because it is the date of the last Treasury auction held before the resolution of the crisis and to avoid the material intraday price movements that happened as the crises was resolved on October 17.

To test for lack of spillover into the benchmark, we ran a regression model with the benchmark as the dependent variable and a debt limit variable that is set to zero for all but the acute period as an exogenous explanatory variable. Setting the variables to zero during the non-acute period helps limit the likelihood of a spurious correlation between the candidate benchmark and the debt limit variables. If either measure, the Google Trends data or the Bloomberg News Trends data, has a statistically significant relationship with the candidate series, we reject it as an appropriate benchmark measure.

To accommodate the time series properties of the benchmark series, we took the first difference of both sides of the regression equation to eliminate the unit root in the benchmark series. To address evidence of generalized autoregressive conditional heteroskedasticity (GARCH) in most of the series, we also estimated a GARCH(1,1) model for the variance term.[48]

The candidate benchmark series that were eliminated at this stage of the testing were:

- LIBOR (overnight, 1- , and 3-month maturities)
- All commercial paper series
- 1-year swaps

In the second stage of testing we identified Treasury-benchmark pairs that are in a long-run equilibrium relationship with the Treasury security. The statistical method we used to identify these pairs, cointegration, has the added benefit of creating a linear combination of the Treasury and benchmark that is stationary, and does not have a unit root.[49] We therefore test for cointegration from the end of the previous debt limit event to the start of the acute period of the debt limit crisis (February 5, 2013 through August 27, 2013), using the Engle-Granger Method for identifying cointegration. If a series is found to be cointegrated with a Treasury maturity, we designate it as an appropriate benchmark for that security for our purposes. The Treasury-benchmark pairs that emerged from these tests are shown in table 3.

Model Fitting Process

With each set of cointegrated pairs, we fit two models, one each for the two proxies we have for the debt limit. For every cointegrated pair, we tailored the lag structures of the main model and the error term through individual testing.[50]

The model estimation followed in two steps. First, we fit a model regressing the Treasury series on its benchmark during the non-acute period. That model was then used to predict Treasury rates during the acute period and error terms for the entire window, February 5, 2013, through October 16, 2013. The resulting error term becomes the dependent variable in the main model.

Table 3. Appropriate Benchmarks Identified For Analysis of Debt Limit Impasse's Effect on Treasury Yields

Treasury Maturity	Appropriate Benchmarks
1-month	Fed Funds LIBOR (6-month and 1-year) Eurodollar rates (1-month and 6-month)
3-month	LIBOR (1-year) Eurodollar rates (6-month)

Table 3. (Continued)

Treasury Maturity	Appropriate Benchmarks
6-month	Fed Funds LIBOR (6-month and 1-year) Eurodollar rates (1-month and 6-month)
1-year	LIBOR (6-month) Eurodollar rates (3-month and 6-month)
2-year	Swaps (2-, 3-, 5-, 7-, 10-, and 30-year)
3-year	Swaps (3- and 5-year)
5-year	Swaps (3-, 5- and 7-year)
7-year	Swaps (5-, 7- and 10-year)
10-year	Swaps (7- and 30-year)
30-year	Swaps (2- and 3-year)

Source: GAO analysis of data from Treasury, the Federal Reserve, and ICE Benchmark Administration. | GAO-15-476

To fit the main model, we followed the following procedure:

1. We used autocorrelations and partial autocorrelations to identify a starting point in testing the autoregressive-moving average (ARMA) lag structure.
2. We tested possible ARMA models, looking at remaining lags in the error term and the statistical significance of the included autoregression terms. Used Information Criteria (IC) statistics if necessary to break ties.
3. We looked for evidence of GARCH disturbances using Engle's Lagrange Multiplier Test.
4. If indicated in step 3 above, we tested GARCH(1,1) and ARCH(1) models using statistical significance and IC tests to determine the appropriate variance structure.

Using this information we identified a preferred model for each Treasury-benchmark pair.

The parameters estimated in the preferred model were then used in the cost analysis described below.

Estimating the Increased Borrowing Costs on Treasury Securities Associated with the 2013 Debt Limit Impasse

For each term and spread, we calculated the difference between total interest paid on Treasury securities auctioned during the debt limit impasse and the interest that we estimate would have been paid through the fiscal year ending on September 30, 2014, in the absence of the debt limit impasse.

For Treasury bills with maturities of less than one year, we calculated the increased borrowing cost, Δ, for a bill auctioned during the debt limit impasse as follows,

$$\Delta I = F \cdot \Delta y \cdot \left(\frac{d}{365}\right) \cdot \left(1 + \frac{y \cdot d}{365}\right)^{-2}.$$

In this formula, F is face value, d is the number of days to maturity, y is the actual bond equivalent yield on the Treasury bill, and Δy is the premium or the change in the yield due to the debt limit impasse.

For 1-year Treasury bills, we calculated the increased borrowing cost, ΔI, for a bill auctioned during the debt limit impasse as follows,

$$\Delta I = F \cdot \Delta y \cdot \left(1 + \frac{y}{2}\right)^{-3} \cdot \frac{days\ to\ 9/30/14}{days\ to\ maturity}.$$

For Treasury notes and bonds, all of which have maturities of 2 years or more, we calculated the annual increased borrowing cost, ΔI_s, for a note or bond auctioned during the debt limit impasse as follows,

$$\Delta I_s = F \cdot \Delta y \cdot \frac{days\ to\ 9/30/14}{days\ to\ maturity}.$$

In our calculations, we set Δy equal to our estimated per-auction premiums, which are calculated thus:

$$\Delta y_t = \hat{\beta}_{debt\ limit} * debt\ limit\ proxy_t$$

We used Constant Maturity Treasury data for the yield on each security. We set d equal to the difference between the maturity date and the issue date from the Treasury auction data. We set F equal to the total face value of securities with accepted bids.

One exception to the approach to calculating the per-auction costs described were auctions where the yields are predicted to have been at or below zero in the absence of the impasse. In these cases we attribute the entire actual interest paid to the debt limit impasse, but no more, since Treasury does not allow Treasury securities to auction at a negative yield.

Selection of Models for Total Cost Calculation

In order to calculate an estimate of the total increased borrowing costs to Treasury as a consequence of the impasse, we selected a suite of models, one for each Treasury maturity. To select the preferred benchmark for each maturity, we used the R-squared statistic from stage 1 of the analysis, which is the stage that cointegrates the Treasury and benchmark pair, and selected the benchmark that produces the highest R-squared statistic.

Results

The following table summarizes the full results of our analysis.

Limitations of Analysis

All regression analyses that attempt to quantify the effect of an event on outcomes are subject to limitations, and this analysis is no exception. Limitations include:

- Our explanatory variables, the Google Trends and Bloomberg News Trends variables, are proxies for the construct of interest—the market consensus estimate of liquidity and/or default risks stemming from the debt limit impasse—and while it is reasonable to think that they correlate with our construct of interest, we cannot empirically test that belief, as the construct itself is not measurable.

- If our explanatory variables are correlated with an event that affects Treasury yields but is not related to the debt limit, our estimates for the costs attributed to the debt limit will be statistically biased.

- Our analysis is not designed to capture long-term costs associated with market perceptions of an increased political risk associated with Treasury securities. Even very small increases in costs that are permanent or long-term could, over time, exceed the acute costs measured here.

- Most of our modeling decisions are based on statistical significance tests, with our cutoffs all set at the 5 percent level. With the large number of tests and models estimated to calculate the costs across the yield curve, there are almost certainly instances in which we exclude results that should be included or include results that should be excluded. As a consequence, the totality of the evidence and the robustness of the results should be considered, in assessing the immediate costs to Treasury of the debt limit impasse, rather than focusing on a single set of point estimates.

- Our model design uses benchmarks to control for changes in interest rates over the period in question that are not due to the debt limit event. To the extent that the benchmarks respond to unrelated events differently than their paired Treasury security does, our estimates will be less precise. If our benchmarks respond to the debt limit impasse in ways not identified by our tests, our estimate of the effects of the impasse on Treasury securities will be biased in the direction of the effect on the benchmark.

- We use the yields in the Constant Maturity Treasury series for all of our calculations to maintain consistency. However, Constant Maturity Treasury data reflect prices at the close of the day on the secondary market, whereas the Treasury auctions are held earlier in the day. Particularly during periods of substantial yield volatility, such as those during the resolution of the debt limit impasse, small differences in the cost calculations could result from intraday price changes.

Table 4. Complete Results for Econometric Models By Treasury Maturity

Treasury	Benchmark	R-squared (1)	ARMA (2)	GARCH (2)	Google Trends Coefficient	Bloomberg News Trends Coefficient (3)	Google Trends Total Costs (4)	Bloomberg News Trends Total Costs (4)
1-month	Eurodollar (1m)	0.418	AR(1)	GARCH(1,1)	0.0541***	10.80***	$11,848,732	$6,776,583
	Eurodollar (6m) (5)	**0.543**	**AR(1)**	**GARCH(1,1)**	**0.0541***	**8.922***	**$11,848,732**	**$5,725,612**
	Fed Funds	0.413	AR(1)	GARCH(1,1)	0.0522***	9.756***	$11,794,281	$6,194,350
	LIBOR (6m)	0.475	AR(1)	GARCH(1,1)	0.0533***	13.89***	$11,848,732	$8,452,196
	LIBOR (1y)	0.476	AR(1)	GARCH(1,1)	0.0538***	14.49***	$11,848,732	$8,692,589
3-month	**Eurodollar (6m)**	**0.682**	**AR(2)**	**ARCH(1)**	**0.00294***	**4.483***		**$9,820,897**
	LIBOR (1y)	0.655	AR(2)	GARCH(1,1)	0.00235**	5.447***	$2,526,947	$11,114,982
6-month	Eurodollar (1m)	0.645	AR(2)	GARCH(1,1)	0.00724***	-4.553***	$25,361,229	$31,155,653
	Eurodollar (6m)	0.707	AR(2)	GARCH(1,1)	0.00601***	-5.186***	$21,027,146	-$28,403,813
	Fed Funds	0.529	AR(1)	GARCH(1,1)	0.00421***	3.784***	$14,744,907	$20,697,227
	LIBOR (6m)	**0.787**	**AR(1)**	**GARCH(1,1)**	**0.00740***	**5.573***	**$25,892,460**	**$30,525,132**
	LIBOR (1y)	0.771	AR(1)	GARCH(1,1)	0.00668***	5.828***	$23,385,595	$31,925,843

Treasury	Benchmark	R-squared (1)	ARMA (2)	GARCH (2)	Google Trends Coefficient	Bloomberg News Trends Coefficient (3)	Google Trends Total Costs (4)	Bloomberg News Trends Total Costs (4)
1-year	Eurodollar (3m)	0.338	AR(1)	—	0.00145**	0.914	$3,848,730	
	Eurodollar (6m)	0.390	AR(1)	—	0.00163***	1.316**	$4,350,469	$3,825,264
	LIBOR (6m)	0.354	AR(2)	—	0.00237***	1.729***	$6,301,184	$5,022,985
2-year	Swap (2y)	0.934	AR(2)	—	0.00227**	2.774***	$1,309,014	$5,208,360
	Swap (3y)	0.923	AR(1)	GARCH(1,1)	0.00119	1.245		
	Swap (5y)	0.885	AR(1)	GARCH(1,1)	-0.00104	-1.143		
	Swap (7y)	0.864	AR(1)	GARCH(1,1)	-0.00153	-1.653		
	Swap (10y)	0.849	AR(1)	GARCH(1,1)	-0.00176	-1.867		
	Swap (30y)	0.792	AR(1)	GARCH(1,1)	-0.00248	-2.869*		
3-year	Swap (3y)	0.984	AR(2)	—	0.00253**	3.674***	$4,435,201	$14,988,619
	Swap (5y)	0.979	AR(2)	ARCH(1)	-0.00279*	-2.550		
5-year	Swap (3y)	0.976	AR(2)	ARCH(1)	-0.00134	-5.089		
	Swap (5y)	0.992	—	—	0.00238	1.990*		
	Swap (7y)	0.991	AR(2)	—	-0.00374	-1.718		
7-year	Swap (5y)	0.985	AR(2)	—	0.00392	6.387*		

Table 4. (Continued)

| | | R-squared | ARMA | GARCH | Google Trends | Bloomberg News Trends | Google Trends | Bloomberg News Trends |
					Coefficient	Coefficient	Total Costs	Total Costs
		(1)	(2)	(2)	(3)	(3)	(4)	(4)
Treasury	**Benchmark**							
	Swap (7y)	0.990	AR(2)	—	0.00235	4.230*		
	Swap (10y)	**0.992**	**AR(2)**	**—**	**-0.00131**	**0.625**		
10-year	Swap (7y)	0.983	AR(3)	GARCH(1,1)	-0.00556	-0.833		
	Swap (30y)	**0.984**	**AR(2)**	**—**	**-0.00826****	**-6.366***	**-$10,235,444**	
30-year	Swap (2y)	0.827	AR(2)	GARCH(1,1)	-0.00256	3.382		
	Swap (3y)	**0.908**	**AR(2)**	**GARCH(1,1)**	**-0.00199**	**2.033**		

Source: GAO analysis of data from Treasury, the Federal Reserve, and ICE Benchmark Administration. | GAO-15-476

Notes:

*** p < 0.01, ** p < 0.05, * p < 0.1

(1) R-squared statistics are from the first step of the analysis where the Treasury series is regressed on the benchmark series in a simple OLS regression.

(2) These two columns list the lag structures for the mean and variance of the second step of the analysis where the error term from the first stage is regressed on a debt limit proxy.

(3) The Bloomberg News Trends coefficient is the estimated coefficient multiplied by 100,000 for ease of reading.

(4) Total cost calculations are estimated total costs incurred through September 30, 2014 for the specified Treasury maturity attributed to the debt limit impasse, if the model's estimated effect is statistically significant at the 5 percent level.

(5) Bolded rows are the preferred benchmark for each Treasury security, chosen for having the largest first stage R-squared statistic of the appropriate benchmarks for that maturity.

APPENDIX III: EXTRAORDINARY MEASURES AVAILABLE TO TREASURY TO MANAGE DEBT WHEN DELAYS IN RAISING THE DEBT LIMIT OCCUR

Table 5. Extraordinary Measures Available to the Department of the Treasury (Treasury) to Manage Debt When Delays in Raising the Debt Limit Occur

Extraordinary measure	Description of extraordinary measure
Suspension of new sales and conversion of demand deposit securities to special 90-day certificates of indebtedness of State and Local Government Series (SLGS) securities	SLGS securities are special securities offered to state and local governments and other issuers of tax-exempt bonds. Suspending new SLGS sales reduces uncertainty over future increases in debt subject to the limit but eliminates a flexible, low-cost option that state and local government issuers have frequently used when refinancing their existing debt before maturity. Converting SLGS demand deposit securities, which increase daily for the interest earned, to special 90-day certificates of indebtedness, which pay interest separately, results in debt subject to the limit not increasing daily for the interest earned.
Suspension of investments to the Government Securities Investment Fund of the Federal Employees' Retirement System (G-Fund)[a]	The G-Fund contains contributions made by federal employees toward their retirement as part of the Thrift Savings Plan program, which are invested in one-day nonmarketable Treasury securities that are subject to the debt limit. If the Secretary determines that the G-Fund may not be fully invested without exceeding the debt limit, Treasury can suspend investments for the entire amount or a portion of the G-Fund on a daily basis to reduce debt subject to the limit. Treasury must notify Congress in writing when the G-Fund cannot be fully invested without exceeding the debt limit. Treasury is required to make the G-Fund whole after the debt limit has been increased.
Suspension of new investments to the Civil Service Retirement and Disability Trust Fund (CSRDF) and Postal Service Retiree Health Benefits Fund (Postal Benefits Fund)[b]	Contributions into the CSRDF (by federal government agencies and their civilian employees toward retirement benefits) and Postal Benefits Fund (by the United States Postal Service toward its retirees' health benefits) are invested in par value nonmarketable Treasury securities that are subject to the debt limit. Treasury is able to suspend new investments to the CSRDF and Postal Benefits Fund if the investment cannot be made without exceeding the debt limit. Treasury must notify Congress in writing when the CSRDF cannot be fully invested without exceeding the debt limit. Treasury is required to make the CSRDF and Postal Benefits

Table 5. (Continued)

Extraordinary measure	Description of extraordinary measure
	Fund whole after the debt issuance suspension period (DISP)—a period in which Treasury determines that it cannot issue debt without exceeding the debt limit—has ended.
Disinvestment of securities held by the CSRDF and Postal Benefits Fund[c]	Treasury is able to disinvest (e.g., redeem earlier than normal) Treasury securities held by the CSRDF and Postal Benefits Fund to prevent the amount of debt from exceeding the debt limit. Treasury must determine that a DISP exists and the length of the DISP, which Treasury uses to determine the amount of investments that can be disinvested. Treasury also must notify Congress in writing when the CSRDF cannot be fully invested without exceeding the debt limit. Treasury is required to make the CSRDF and Postal Benefits Fund whole after the DISP has ended.
Suspension of Exchange	The ESF is used to help provide a stable system of monetary exchange rates. Dollar- denominated assets of
Stabilization Fund (ESF) investments	the ESF not used for program purposes are generally invested in one- day nonmarketable Treasury securities that are subject to the debt limit. When debt approaches the limit, Treasury can suspend investment for the entire amount or a portion of the ESF's maturing nonmarketable Treasury securities. Treasury lacks legislative authority to restore lost interest to the ESF when the debt limit is increased.
Exchanging Federal Financing Bank (FFB) debt for debt subject to the limit	FFB is a government corporation under the general supervision and direction of the Secretary of the Treasury, which borrows from the Treasury to finance purchases of agency debt and agency guaranteed debt. It can also issue up to $15 billion of its own debt—FFB 9(a) obligations—that is not subject to the debt limit. This debt can be exchanged with other federal debt (e.g., securities held by the CSRDF) to reduce the amount of debt subject to the limit.

Source: GAO analysis of related legislation and regulations. | GAO-15-476
[a] 5 U.S.C. §§ 8438(g), (h).
[b] 5 U.S.C. §§ 8348(j), (l) and 5 U.S.C. § 8909a(c).
[c] 5 U.S.C. §§ 8348(k), (l) and 5 U.S.C. § 8909a(c).

APPENDIX IV: CHRONOLOGY OF EVENTS RELATED TO THE DEBT LIMIT, FEBRUARY 2013 THROUGH FEBRUARY 2014

Table 6. Chronology of Events Related to the Debt Limit, February 2013 through February 2014

Date	Event
February 4, 2013	The President signed No Budget, No Pay Act of 2013 (Pub. L. No. 113-3) into law, suspending the debt limit until May 19, 2013.
May 17, 2013	The Secretary of the Department of the Treasury (Treasury) sent a letter to Congress stating that Treasury's estimates indicated
	that extraordinary measures would not be exhausted until after Labor Day (September 2, 2013). Treasury began suspending new sales of State and Local Government Series (SLGS) securities.
May 19, 2013	As authorized by the No Budget, No Pay Act of 2013, the debt limit was reinstated at $16.699 trillion to accommodate debt incurred to pay obligations during the suspension period.
May 20, 2013	The Secretary of the Treasury notified Congress that he had determined a debt issuance suspension period (DISP)[a] existed from May 20,2013, until August 2, 2013, and Treasury (1) redeemed a portion of investments held by the Civil Service Retirement and Disability Trust Fund (CSRDF) earlier than normal and (2) began suspending new investments to the CSRDF and Postal Service Retiree Health Benefits Fund (Postal Benefits Fund).
May 31, 2013	The Secretary of the Treasury notified Congress that he would be unable to fully invest the Government Securities Investment Fund of the Federal Employees' Retirement System (G-Fund), and Treasury began suspending investments to the G-Fund.
August 2, 2013	The Secretary of the Treasury notified Congress that he determined that the DISP previously declared would be extended until October 11, 2013.
August 26, 2013	The Secretary of the Treasury notified Congress that Treasury projected that extraordinary measures would be exhausted by the middle of October 2013, and that at that time Treasury would have $50 billion cash on hand.

Table 6. (Continued)

Date	Event
September 25, 2013	The Secretary of the Treasury sent a letter to Congress stating that Treasury's updated estimates indicated that extraordinary measures would be exhausted no later than October 17, 2013, and that at that date Treasury would have $30 billion cash on hand.
October 1, 2013	The Secretary of the Treasury notified Congress that he determined that the previously declared DISP would be extended until October 17, 2013, and Treasury (1) began suspending daily reinvestments of Exchange Stabilization Fund (ESF) investments, and (2) entered into a debt swap with the Federal Financing Bank (FFB) and CSRDF. The Secretary of the Treasury reiterated Treasury's earlier estimates that extraordinary measures would be exhausted no later than October 17, 2013, and that at that time Treasury would have $30 billion cash on hand.
	The federal government partially shut down due to a lapse in appropriations, requiring agencies without available funds to cease all operations with few exceptions, such as the protection of human life and property.
October 10, 2013	The Secretary of the Treasury testified before the Senate Finance Committee and restated Treasury's earlier estimates that extraordinary measures would be exhausted no later than October 17, 2013.
October 17, 2013	The President signed the Continuing Appropriations Act, 2014 (Pub. L. No. 113-46) into law, suspending the debt limit through February 7, 2014 and funding the government through January 15, 2014.[b] Treasury restored all uninvested principal of the CSRDF and Postal Benefits Fund.[c]
January 22, 2014	The Secretary of the Treasury sent a letter to the Senate and House Majority and Minority Leaders stating that Treasury's updated estimates indicated that extraordinary measures would be exhausted in late February.
February 7, 2014	The Secretary of the Treasury notified Congress of the upcoming reinstatement of the debt limit and stated that Treasury's updated estimates indicated that extraordinary measures would not last beyond February 27, 2014. Treasury began suspending new issuances of SLGS securities.

Date	Event
February 8, 2014	As authorized by the Continuing Appropriations Act, 2014, the debt limit was reinstated at $17.212 trillion to accommodate debt incurred to pay obligations during the suspension period.
February 10, 2014	The Secretary of the Treasury notified Congress that he had determined a DISP existed from February 10,2014, until February 27, 2014. Treasury began suspending new investments to the CSRDF and to the G-Fund.
February 15, 2014	The President signed the Temporary Debt Limit Extension Act (Pub. L. No 113-83) into law, suspending the debt limit through March 15, 2015.

Source: GAO analysis of congressional actions and documentation from Treasury. | GAO-15-476

Notes:

[a] A debt issuance suspension period is a period in which Treasury determines that it cannot issue debt without exceeding the debt limit. Treasury must determine that a debt issuance suspension period exists and the length of the period in order to use certain extraordinary measures.

[b] The Consolidated Appropriations Act, 2014, enacted on January 17, 2014, provided funding for the remainder of fiscal year 2014.

[c] Treasury did not restore interest losses to the Exchange Stabilization Fund because it lacks legislative authority to do so.

End Notes

[1] GAO, *Debt Limit: Analysis of 2011-2012 Actions Taken and Effect of Delayed Increase on Borrowing Costs*, GAO-12-701 (Washington, D.C.: July 23, 2012), and *Debt Limit: Delays Create Debt Management Challenges and Increase Uncertainty in the Treasury Market*, GAO-11-203 (Washington, D.C.: Feb. 22, 2011).

[2] Pub. L. No. 113-46, § 1002, 127 Stat. 558, 566–570.

[3] For example, a recent study used Google search data to estimate the perceived risk of a breakup of the euro area on the yields for European sovereign debt. See Cesare, Antonio Di, Giuseppe Grande, Michele Manna and Marco Taboga, "Recent Estimates of Sovereign Risk Premia for Euro-Area Countries," *Questioni di Economia e Finanza* Occasional Papers, No. 128, (2012). Google search data have also been used to predict search data to predict upcoming economic data releases for U.S. retail sales, auto sales, home sales, and foreclosures in the United States. In addition, U.S. federal agencies have also used Google search data. Most notably, Google search data was used by researchers at the Centers for Disease Control and Prevention and Google to estimate the current level of weekly influenza activity in different regions of the United States. See Ginsberg, Jeremy, Matthew H. Mohebbi, Rajan S. Patel, Lynnette Brammer, Mark S. Smolinski and Larry Brilliant, "Detecting Influenza Epidemics Using Search Engine Query Data," *Nature*, vol. 457, no.19 (2009).

[4] GAO-12-701 and GAO-11-203.

[5] Pub. L. No. 77-7, 55 Stat. 7 (Feb. 19, 1941).

[6] For additional information on federal debt and debt subject to the limit, see GAO, "Fiscal Outlook: Understanding the Federal Debt," *Key Issues*, (Washington, D.C.: 2014), accessed June 23, 2015, http://www.gao.gov/fiscal_outlook/understanding_federal_debt/overview and GAO, *Financial Audit: Bureau of the Fiscal Service's Fiscal Years 2014 and 2013 Schedules of Federal Debt*, GAO-15-157 (Washington, D.C.: Nov. 10, 2014).

[7] Prior to November 2008, Treasury maintained a majority of its operating cash as short term investments with commercial depositaries. From December 2008 to December 2011, Treasury maintained approximately $2 billion as investments with commercial depositaries.

[8] Whether or not Treasury can draw down on its operating cash balance depends on both the level of Treasury's current cash balance and on what Treasury's payment obligations are. Treasury must maintain an adequate cash balance in its account at the Federal Reserve Bank of New York to accommodate large swings in daily deposits and withdrawals. Treasury cannot risk an overdraft because the Federal Reserve is not authorized to lend to Treasury.

[9] 5 U.S.C. § 8348(j), (l).

[10] For a more detailed description of each the extraordinary measures available and how Treasury has used these measures during past debt limit impasses, see GAO-12-701 and GAO-11-203.

[11] Pub. L. No. 112-25, § 301, 125 Stat. 240, 251–255 (Aug. 2, 2011), *codified at* 31 U.S.C. §§ 3101 and 3101A.

[12] For a chronology of the significant events leading up to the August 2, 2011, debt limit increase and related information, see GAO-12-701.

[13] Pub. L. No. 113-3, § 2, 127 Stat. 51, 51 (Feb. 4, 2013).

[14] Treasury suspended the use of State and Local Government Series (SLGS) securities on May 17, 2013. While the amount of funds borrowed through SLGS is relatively small compared to the amount of marketable securities issued, the timing of the funds flow from these sources is generally out of Treasury's control, and Treasury normally suspends the sale of SLGS during a debt limit impasse since it is the largest source of volatility among non-marketable borrowing from the public.

[15] If one or more appropriations acts are not enacted at the start of the fiscal year, federal agencies may lack sufficient funding to legally incur new obligations and may be forced to shut down. In contrast, a failure to raise the debt limit does not force federal agencies to shut down, as federal agencies are still legally authorized to incur new obligations. However, a delay in raising the debt limit could impede Treasury's ability to make timely payments to grantees, contractors, federal employees, and other recipients of federal funding for those legally incurred obligations.

[16] Pub. L. No. 113-46, 127 Stat. 558. The Consolidated Appropriations Act, 2014, enacted on January 17, 2014, provided funding for the remainder of fiscal year 2014.

[17] The amount outstanding includes both (1) the principal payments due in late October through mid-November 2013 and (2) the principal on Treasury notes and bonds with scheduled coupon payments during this time period that do not fully mature until a later date.

[18] For fixed income securities like Treasury securities, price and yield move inversely to each other. When market interest rates rise, prices of fixed income securities fall.

[19] 17 C.F.R. § 270.2a-7(f). If a default occurs, the money market fund must dispose of the defaulted security as soon as practicable, consistent with achieving an orderly disposition of the security absent a finding by the board of directors that disposal of the portfolio security would not be in the best interests of the money market fund. Such a determination may take into account, among other factors, market conditions that could affect the orderly disposition of the portfolio security.

[20] Twenty-two banks and securities broker-dealers are currently designated by the Federal Reserve Bank of New York as primary dealers and are expected to participate meaningfully in every Treasury auction by bidding for, at a minimum, an amount of securities representing their share of the offered amount (based on the number of primary dealers at the time of the auction). Primary dealers also have a role in making a secondary market for

Treasury securities—the market in which previously issued Treasury marketable securities are bought and sold among investors.

[21] The Federal Reserve Bank of New York publishes monthly data on the market value of tri-party and GCF repurchase agreements. The data are generally as of the seventh business day of the month, which is meant to represent a typical business day, as data on certain dates, such as the first or last day of the month or settlement dates for certain securities, could lead to distortions in the data.

[22] Data are not seasonally adjusted. Data for non-financial and asset-backed commercial paper outstanding did not show a similar decline.

[23] The TMPG is a group of market professionals committed to supporting the integrity and efficiency of the Treasury, agency debt, and agency mortgage-backed securities markets. The TMPG is composed of senior business managers and legal and compliance professionals from a variety of institutions, including securities dealers, banks, buy-side firms, market utilities, and others, and is sponsored by the Federal Reserve Bank of New York.

[24] The TMPG white paper noted that delayed payment on Treasury debt could arise from a number of circumstances, such as systems failures, natural disasters, terrorist acts, or other reasons.

[25] The Federal Reserve's Fedwire Securities Service provides safekeeping, transfer, and settlement services for securities issued by Treasury and other federal agencies. Fedwire Securities Service ordinarily runs its end-of-day processes following the close of the service (at around 7 p.m. Eastern time). Among other things, these processes include making securities due to mature the next day non-transferrable through the Fedwire Securities Service.

[26] On July 13, 2011, Moody's Investors Service placed the United States' credit rating on review for a possible downgrade. See Moody's Investors Service, *Moody's Places US Aaa Government Bond Rating and Related Ratings on Review for Possible Downgrade* (July, 13, 2011). On July 14, 2011, Standard & Poor's placed the long- and short-term credit ratings of the United States on CreditWatch, indicating a substantial likelihood of it taking a rating action within the next 90 days. See Standard & Poor's, *United States of America 'AAA/A-1+' Ratings Placed On CreditWatch Negative On Rising Risk Of Policy Stalemate* (July, 14, 2011). On August 5, 2011, Standard & Poor's lowered its long-term sovereign credit rating on the United States from AAA to AA+. Standard & Poor's indicated at the time the prolonged debate over raising the debt limit in 2011 contributed to its decision. See Standard & Poor's *United States of America Long-Term Rating Lowered To 'AA+' Due to Political Risks, Rising Debt Burden; Outlook Negative* (Aug. 5, 2011).

[27] We used an econometric model to analyze the association between measures of public interest or concern over the debt limit impasse and deviations from predicted Treasury yields relative to relevant benchmarks. We then translated those regression estimates of yield increases to interest costs attributable to the debt limit at each Treasury auction held from February 5, 2013, to October 16, 2013.

[28] None of our models showed statistically significant costs for Treasury securities with maturities of 5-years or more. In one set of specifications, we estimated a statistically significant savings for 10-year notes.

[29] GAO-12-701 and GAO-11-203.

[30] This is based on our model that uses Google Trends as an explanatory variable, which produces the lower estimate of total increased borrowing costs.

[31] No Budget, No Pay Act of 2013, Pub. L. No. 113-3, § 2, 127 Stat. 51, 51 (Feb. 4, 2013); Continuing Appropriations Act, 2014, Pub. L. No. 113-46, § 1002, 127 Stat. 558, 566–567 (Oct. 17, 2013); and Temporary Debt Limit Extension Act, Pub. L. No 113-83, § 2, 128 Stat. 1011, 1011 (Feb. 15, 2014).

[32] Pub. L. No. 111-203, 124 Stat. 1376 (July 21, 2010).

[33] Rollover risk includes two types of risk: (1) interest rate risk—the risk that Treasury will have to refinance its debt at less favorable interest rates, and (2) market access risk—the risks inherent in coming back to the market to refinance the debt.

[34] GAO, *Standards for Internal Control in the Federal Government*, GAO/AIMD-00-21.3.1 (Washington, D.C.: Nov.1,1999) and *Government Operations: Standards for Internal Control in the Federal Government*, GAO-14-704G (Washington, D.C.: Sept. 10, 2014).

[35] See GAO-12-701 and GAO-11-203.

[36] A similar House rule was used for increasing the debt limit in the 97th through 101st Congresses and the 108th through 111th Congresses. Most recently, this was House Rule XXVIII in the 111th Congress. A similar provision was not included in the House Rules for the 112th, 113th, or 114th Congresses.

[37] The Congressional Budget and Impoundment Control Act of 1974 also allows for the debt limit to be raised through reconciliation. Reconciliation is a process that Congress can use to make adjustments to existing laws affecting tax, spending, credit, and the debt limit so they are consistent with the levels set in the budget resolution. Unlike the budget resolution, reconciliation legislation is presented to the President and, if signed, has the force of law. One advantage of using reconciliation is that it is subject to expedited consideration in both chambers. In the Senate, for example, debate on reconciliation legislation is limited, making it more difficult to filibuster. In the last 30 years, reconciliation has been used four times to increase the debt limit—most recently in 1997.

[38] Statutory Pay-As-You-Go Act of 2010, Pub. L. No. 111-139, 124 Stat. 8, 8 (Feb. 12, 2010).

[39] House and Senate budget rules are typically enforced through a point of order, which can be waived by a majority vote in the House and generally by a three-fifths vote in the Senate.

[40] Pub. L. No. 110-289, § 3083, 122 Stat. 2654, 2908 (July 30, 2008); Pub. L. No. 110-343, § 122, 122 Stat. 3765, 3790 (Oct. 3, 2008); Pub. L. No. 111-5, § 1604, 123 Stat. 115, 366 (Feb. 17, 2009).

[41] The President is required to submit an update of the federal budget, often referred to as a mid-session review, before July 16 of each year. 31 U.S.C. § 1106.

[42] GAO-11-203.

[43] Congress reached agreement on budget procedures in the Balanced Budget and Emergency Deficit Control Act of 1985, Pub. L. No. 99-177, 99 Stat. 1038 (Dec. 12, 1985); Balanced Budget and Emergency Deficit Control Reaffirmation Act of 1987, Pub. L. No. 100-119, 101 Stat. 754 (Sept. 29, 1987), Budget Enforcement Act of 1990, Pub. L. No. 101-508, title XIII, 104 Stat. 1388, 1388–573 to 1388–630 (Nov. 5, 1990); title XIV of the Omnibus Budget Reconciliation Act of 1993, Pub. L. No. 103-66, §§ 14001–14014, 107 Stat. 312, 683 (Aug. 10, 1993), Budget Enforcement Act of 1997, Pub. L. No. 105-33, 111 Stat. 251 (Aug. 5, 1997), Statutory Pay-As-You-Go Act of 2010, Pub. L. No. 111-139, 124 Stat. 8 (Feb. 12, 2010); and BCA, Pub. L. No. 112-25, 125 Stat. 240 (Aug. 2, 2011).

[44] GAO-12-701 and GAO-11-203.

[45] It is important that the benchmark not experience spillover effects from the debt limit impasse on its own prices so that it can help model what Treasury yields would have been in the absence of the impasse.

[46] For example, a recent study used Google search data to estimate the perceived risk of a breakup of the euro area on the yields for European sovereign debt. See Cesare, Antonio Di, Giuseppe Grande, Michele Manna and Marco Taboga, "Recent Estimates of Sovereign Risk Premia for Euro-Area Countries," *Questioni di Economia e Finanza* Occasional Papers, No. 128, (2012). Google search data have also been used to predict search data to predict upcoming economic data releases for U.S. retail sales, auto sales, home sales, and foreclosures in the United States. In addition, U.S. federal agencies have also used Google search data. Most notably, Google search data was used by researchers at the Centers for Disease Control and Prevention and Google to estimate the current level of weekly influenza activity in different regions of the United States. See Ginsberg, Jeremy, Matthew H. Mohebbi, Rajan S. Patel, Lynnette Brammer, Mark S. Smolinski and Larry Brilliant,

"Detecting Influenza Epidemics Using Search Engine Query Data," *Nature*, vol. 457, no.19 (2009).

[47] We determined that sufficient coverage was obtained using just two search terms. In comparison, we found that Google search criteria needed be defined more broadly for our purposes.

[48] Some of the models fail to converge with a GARCH(1,1) specification, so we tailor their variance terms individually.

[49] A unit root is a statistical property of some time series data that violates the assumptions of ordinary least squares regression analysis (OLS) and introduces substantial risk of spurious but statistically significant results. If the conditions of cointegration are met, however, the presence of the unit roots can be leveraged to produce super-consistent OLS estimates that are more precise.

[50] The explanatory variable used generally has no material effect on the lag structures tested. In borderline cases, we explore more thoroughly the test statistics from both models to aid in selecting the preferred lag structure.

INDEX

influenza a, 117, 120
information technology, 82
institutions, 18, 46, 49, 60, 64, 68, 69, 80,
    81, 93, 101, 119
integrity, 119
interest rates, 29, 58, 61, 98, 109, 118, 120
intervention, 72
investment(s), vii, 1, 3, 5, 7, 9, 10, 11, 15,
    26, 28, 30, 32, 33, 34, 38, 40, 41, 46, 55,
    5, 81, 113, 114, 115, 116, 117, 118
investors, 19, 20, 29, 30, 45, 46, 49, 58, 59,
    60, 61, 62, 64, 68, 69, 74, 75, 93, 119
issues, 5, 13, 20, 21, 30, 31, 38, 47, 48, 52,
    54, 72, 80, 81, 84, 86, 97

J

journalists, 51, 103

K

Kagan, Elena, 14, 36

L

laws, 37, 45, 56, 57, 79, 84, 91, 92, 120
lead, 18, 20, 50, 69, 83, 95, 119
legislation, 2, 4, 21, 22, 23, 24, 30, 39, 41,
    44, 48, 49, 52, 72, 83, 85, 86, 87, 88, 89,
    90, 91, 92, 93, 97, 114, 120
legislative authority, 114, 117
lending, 58
light, 48, 92
liquid assets, 81
liquidate, vii, 3, 12, 14, 16
liquidity, 45, 49, 58, 61, 62, 68, 74, 81, 99,
    108
loans, 58
local government, 3, 5, 37, 54, 113
logistics, 73
low risk, 64

M

majority, 30, 34, 54, 118, 120
management, 2, 5, 7, 15, 26, 27, 32, 35, 38,
    43, 48, 49, 50, 55, 56, 78, 80, 81, 82, 83,
    91, 92, 93, 94, 95, 97
market access, 82, 83, 120
materials, 51, 103
matter, 37
Medicaid, 37
Medicare, 4, 7, 15, 27, 32, 54, 80
methodology, 52, 53, 75
military, 30
model specification, 99
models, 51, 52, 53, 75, 78, 96, 98, 99, 101,
    105, 106, 108, 109, 119, 121
modifications, 91
monetary policy, 81
money markets, 17
mortgage-backed securities, 119
Moses, 39

N

national debt, 29
natural disaster(s), 46, 119
negative consequences, 17, 24, 29
New Zealand, 91
nutrition, 88

O

Obama Administration, 20, 29
Obama, President Barack, 20, 22, 29, 32, 39
Office of Management and Budget (OMB),
    11, 13, 14, 21, 33, 35, 36, 39, 48, 52, 97
officials, 7, 12, 15, 27, 36, 43, 50, 53, 72,
    73, 81, 96, 97
operations, vii, 1, 3, 8, 10, 20, 26, 28, 30,
    37, 41, 50, 55, 56, 83, 116
optimism, 18
oversight, 44, 48, 84, 92, 93

T

U